gay *by the* bay

gay *by the* bay

A History of Queer Culture in the San Francisco Bay Area

by Susan Stryker and
Jim Van Buskirk
FOREWORD BY ARMISTEAD MAUPIN

CHRONICLE BOOKS
SAN FRANCISCO

Library of Congress Cataloging-in-Publication Data:
Susan Stryker.
            Gay by the Bay : a history of queer culture
    in the San Francisco Bay Area / Susan Stryker & Jim Van Buskirk.
            p.   cm.
            Includes bibliographical references (p.) and index.
    ISBN 0-8118-1187-5 (pbk.)
    1. Homosexuality—California—San Francisco Metropolitan
    Area—History. 2. Gays—California—San Francisco Metropolitan Area
    —History. 3. San Francisco Metropolitan Area (Calif.)—History.
I. Van Buskirk, Jim. II. Title.
HQ76.3.U52s267   1996
306. 76'6'7946—dc20   95-36093
                                              CIP
Printed in Hong Kong.

ISBN: 0-8118-1187-5

Cover and book design by Brenda Rae Eno
Front cover photograph credits (left to right):
Brenda Eno, Courtesy of GLHS, photograph of Justin Bond
by Daniel Nicoletta, Crawford Barton.
Back cover photograph credits (left to right):
Rink Foto, Courtesy of Bancroft Library/University of California at Berkeley,
Daniel Nicoletta, Crawford Barton.
Page one: Photograph by Daniel Nicoletta.

Distributed in Canada by
Raincoast Books
8680 Cambie Street
Vancouver, B.C. V6P 6M9

10 9 8 7 6 5 4 3 2 1

Chronicle Books
275 Fifth Street
San Francisco, CA 94103

Contents

Acknowledgments

This book seems to have led a charmed life since the moment of its casual, unplanned conception during an idle conversation between the authors one June afternoon in 1994, following an AIDS History Project board meeting on the UCSF campus.

When we sat down several weeks later to think about the book more seriously, we immediately agreed on who we most wanted to publish it—Chronicle Books, whose handsomely printed volumes and local roots made them the logical choice for the lavishly illustrated volume we envisioned. We were quite pleased with the enthusiasm with which Chronicle greeted our proposal, and the subsequent process of bringing the book to press with them has done nothing to lessen that initial pleasure. We'd like to thank all the people at Chronicle Books whose interest in and support of this project has made our work so enjoyable—associate publisher Caroline Herter; Janet Saevitz, who first brought our project to the attention of Chronicle Books and has since participated in numerous ways; Craig Hetzer, who has handled all the practical details of publishing a book; graphic designer Brenda Eno; and project editor Terry Ryan.

We thought Armistead Maupin would be the ideal person to pen a few opening words for the book, and we were right. Though neither of us knew him, we needn't have felt intimidated by his international reputation—Armistead provided helpful suggestions in addition to a charming foreword to the book.

Once we began the hard work of researching, writing, and actually producing the book, we found Alyson Belcher to be an indispensible collaborator. Originally hired as the photographic assistant, we quickly came to appreciate not only her skill with the camera, but also her archival training and her familiarity with the source material of Bay Area queer history. She alerted us to many important collections in the Bancroft Library at UC Berkeley. Bill Walker, cofounder of the Gay and Lesbian Historical Society of Northern California, also lent his considerable expertise as the archival consultant to this project. Gayle Rubin graciously opened her private archive of S/M-related materials to us, and photographers Cathy Cade, Rick Gerharter, Dan Nicoletta, and Rink shared their extensive collections of documentary images. Professor Nan Alamilla Boyd of the University of Colorado generously allowed us to consult her unpublished manuscript, *San Francisco Was a Wide Open Town,* a history of Bay Area lesbian and gay communities between 1945 and 1965, soon to be published by the University of California Press.

People too numerous to mention by name helped out with specific aspects of the research, but the following (in no particular order) deserve special recognition: Lisbet Tellefsen for help with African American sources; Gray Brechin for his research on Douglas Tilden; Jeffrey A. Barr, Librarian at the California Historical Society; Dorr Jones for his reminiscence of Douglass Cross and George Cory; Eric Garber for being a fount of pertinent information; Greg Pennington for some useful chronologies of important events in the 1960s and 1970s; Gerard Koskovich for his detailed knowledge of Stanford University alumni; Stuart Timmons for supplying a photo of Harry Hay; Jordy Jones for information on the 1995 police raid on the Visual Aid benefit; Jim Gordon and Will Roscoe for steering us toward useful Native American sources. We thank Julie Pavlowski and Dan Cuny at Faulkner Photo Lab for their calm professionalism, and Loren Cameron for taking our authors' portraits. Wilson Westbrook-Fergeson saved the day with some emergency data restoration after an untimely disk crash. Pat Holt helped ferry the manuscript to and from authors and editors. Frank Free, courtesy of our membership in the National Writer's Union, offered advice on contract negotiations, as did Elizabeth Pomada, while Brian Ferrall advised us on permissions to reproduce graphic material. We would also like to thank the staff of the San Francisco History Room of the San Francisco Public Library—Pat Akre (whose assistance with photographs was invaluable), Stan Carroll, and Michael Sherrod-Flores.

Several people read and commented upon the manuscript in whole or in part and made valuable suggestions: Ruth Mahaney, Daniel Bao, Lisbet Tellefsen, Bill Walker, and Kim Toevs. Their input is greatly appreciated. Of course, we are responsible for any errors, factual or interpretive.

This book literally would not have been possible without the research of an entire generation of scholars who have amassed and interpreted the records of San Francisco's queer past. We feel especially indebted to the path-breaking work of John D'Emilio, Allan Bérubé, and the members of the San Francisco Lesbian and Gay History Project. We are also indebted to the countless volunteers and members who have kept the Gay and Lesbian Historical Society (GLHS) of Northern California functioning since 1985. To honor this underappreciated service to the community, we are donating a portion our royalties to the GLHS, as well as to the Gay and Lesbian Center at the San Francisco New Main Public Library.

Jim would like to personally acknowledge the encouraging support of Maxine Shear, Bill Hayes, Carse McDaniel, and Rob Lieber, while Susan would like to thank Aileen Dover for making home such a stimulating place.

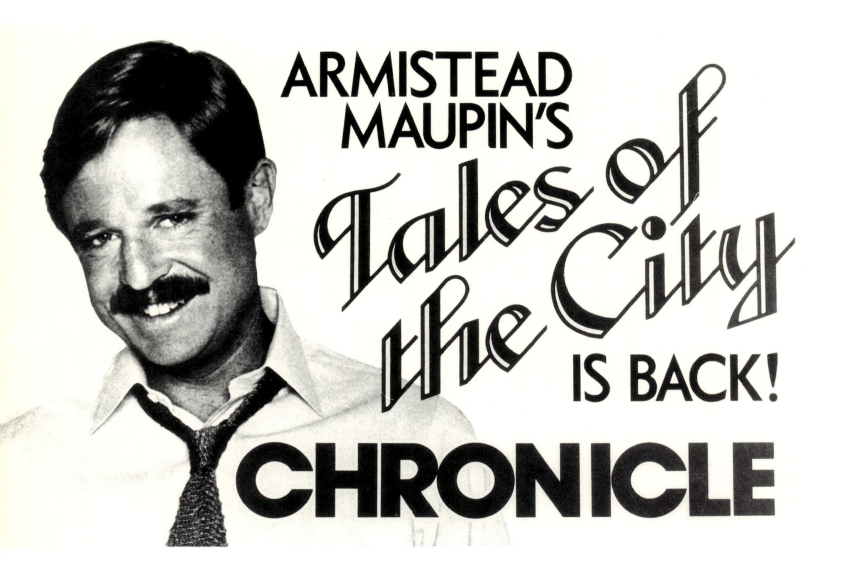

ARMISTEAD
MAUPIN'S
*Tales of
the City*
IS BACK!

CHRONICLE

Foreword

BY ARMISTEAD MAUPIN

On April 22, 1979, after a century of speculation, the day had finally come for a time capsule to be exhumed from the base of a statue in Washington Square. It was raining hard, but nearly a thousand San Franciscans stood in rapt silence as Mayor Dianne Feinstein snipped open an 18-inch lead cube to reveal what treasures had been entombed there in 1879.

The ceremony held a special significance for me. My recently published novel, *Tales of the City,* was to be interred that day in a new capsule, earmarked for the citizens of 2079, along with such items as a pair of Levis, a poem by Lawrence Ferlinghetti, a bottle of Cabernet Sauvignon, and a record by the Hoodoo Rhythm Devils. I remember feeling proud that I'd contributed something to the future that was unapologetically queer. I didn't count on being upstaged by something from the past.

Most of the items from the 1879 capsule turned out to be disappointingly bland: a string of buttons, various temperance tracts, a dress catalog, assorted photographs, newspapers, a fork. But a modest pamphlet entitled *The Great Geysers of California, and How to Reach Them* by Laura De Force Gordon offered an intriguing bonus. Scribbled on its flyleaf in a spidery Victorian hand was this message:

> *If this little book should see the light after its 100 years of entombment, I would like its readers to know that the author was a lover of her own sex and devoted the best years of her life in striving for the political equality and social and moral elevation of woman.*

"A lover of her own sex"? Was Laura De Force Gordon trying to tell us something? Was she coming out in another century because she couldn't do it in her own? Or was that phrase, as some have suggested, merely an idiosyncrasy of 19th-century speech? Either way, I felt a curious kinship with the woman behind that lovely, yet satisfyingly sturdy name. I pictured her in her tailored tweeds and a wide-brimmed hat, striding through a thicket with another Geyser Gal on her arm. Could she have ever imagined that a woman mayor would open the time capsule? Or that one day gay people would become a major political force in San Francisco?

The matter of Ms. Gordon's sexuality may always be a mystery, and that is nothing new. Two thousand years of Judeo-Christian suppression have made gay people the world's most invisible population. Our lives and dreams and contributions have been systematically obliterated— sometimes at our own hand, sometimes at the hand of others. Until very recently, proof of our existence could be found only in court records and journals of pathology. It took a new breed of archivists, openly gay and actively curious, to begin the process of excavating our past.

Witness this book, the first-ever effort at compiling a queer history of San Francisco. It tells a remarkable story that spans two centuries—from the cross-dressing practices of Indians at the Mission Dolores to the signing of a municipal transgender rights law in 1995. The story is all the more compelling because it isn't driven by war or money or politics—the way most histories are—but by the basic human need to find love and self-fulfillment. It's a chronicle of quiet courage and noisy protest, one so richly varied that it transcends the usual boundaries of race, class, and religion.

For a while now, the press has dubbed San Francisco the "Gay Capital of the World," a label most of us wear as a badge of honor. This city has long been the cradle of American cultural change—from Bohemians to beats to hippies to hackers—so it was probably always destined to lead the century's last great fight for human rights. Though conventional lore dates the modern gay movement from New York's Stonewall Uprising of 1969, a quick glance at this book reveals a more complicated truth: San Francisco activists were scrapping with police—and even running for office—years before anyone thought to pick up a rock in Sheridan Square.

Never mind. We're a small town, really, and we're used to seeing others take our "wacky" ideas and run with them. It's enough to know that the values of freedom and tolerance nurtured for so long in this beautiful place have sooner or later helped change the minds of people everywhere. It's certainly enough for me, and I expect it would be for Laura De Force Gordon.

Introduction

If San Francisco's status as the "Gay Capital of the World" was secured by the time *Life* magazine featured photos of two local gay bars in its 1964 article "Homosexuality in America," the city's history as a queer place began long before that. Because the greater San Francisco Bay Area has been at the forefront of artistic, political, social, cultural, and sexual queer activity since World War II—and has queer roots stretching back into the 19th century—it is surprising that there has never before been a book-length chronicle of this "gay mecca." With *Gay by the Bay,* we feel we have taken an important step toward telling the exciting story of what lesbians, bisexuals, transgendered people, and gay men in the Bay Area have accomplished.

Because words are such slippery, shape-changing beasts, we've tried to address the problem of shifting terminology in a number of different ways. When we chose to use the word "gay" in our title, for example, we intended it in the older sense that referred to both men and women. We intended the word "queer" in its most inclusive sense, too. We use "queer" to describe all those whose sexual orientation or gender identification deviated from an ever-evolving norm, rather than repetitively employ the currently mandatory but stylistically awkward litany of "gay, lesbian, bisexual, and transgender." We realize that "queer" has had very specific (and often derogatory) meanings over the years, and that its present usage often provokes controversy. Still, there seems no better single word that captures the broad range of identities, practices, lifestyles, orientations, genders, and sexualities that we seek to describe. Sometimes our terminology undoubtedly appears unsettlingly anachronistic, but we trust that readers will understand our intent. In other instances, we use words no longer current ("homophile") when those words were used by people to describe themselves in the historical period under discussion.

"Community," another word we use frequently in this book, presents its own difficulties. There has never been one monolithic queer community in the Bay Area. Rather, there is a bewildering variety of intersecting subcultural scenes, separatist enclaves, political factions, ethnicities, genders, and classes. By speaking of *the* Bay Area queer community in this book, we are not seeking to deny the seriousness and complexity of these many divisions, or to pretend that we are representing the full diversity of queer lives and histories. We do mean to suggest, however, that living in the same geographical location creates a set of overlapping experiences within local queer cultures.

We've aimed for breadth of coverage in this book rather than depth, but there is one area that we feel is lacking—graphic representations of explicitly sexual material. Sexuality occupies a unique role in queer culture, because it is in terms of our sexual identity that we mark ourselves as different from the dominant society—and are marked by others as a deviant and marginalized social group. Each of us wanted to include images of queer people enjoying their bodies. We reluctantly chose not to include photographic representations of erotic practices, however, but to describe the social and cultural significance of queer passion and document the scenes where it is played out. We made our decision partly in response to the repressive political climate here in the United States, and to the censorship laws in various English-speaking countries. Because we feel the story we're relating is an important one, we chose the representational practice that could reach the widest audience without diluting the content of what we wanted to say.

We by no means feel we've exhausted the subject of San Francisco's queer history—in fact we've barely scratched the surface. Attempting to adequately document the long span of years between the 1840s and the 1990s, even limited to a specific geographic region, has proven challenging. Many of the events, organizations, and individuals that we omitted entirely or mentioned only in passing merit in-depth attention. We think of this volume as an initial sketch, a rough map of the past as it presents itself to us from our particular late-20th-century vantage points. We hope that future historians will find in the Gay Bay a tempting invitation to uncover more of the rich history of queer people in the San Francisco Bay Area.

In the course of our research, we became reacquainted with many favorite and familiar aspects of the Bay Area's queer culture, while also uncovering much that was surprising and new to us. We hope you have a similar experience as you explore *Gay by the Bay.*

gay *by the* bay

"It's an odd thing, but everyone who disappears is said to be seen at San Francisco. It must be a delightful city, and possess all the attractions of the next world."

—**Oscar Wilde,**
Picture of Dorian Gray (1891)

Oscar Wilde.
Courtesy of Gay & Lesbian Historical Society of Northern California (GLHS).

An Odd Thing:

Homosexual History before World War II

Two short anecdotes suggest how queer a place California has seemed to the people who have come here as colonizers and immigrants ever since the 16th century.

The first anecdote has to do with the name "California" itself: It derives from a fanciful description of an island of Amazon women. Although the name seems to have been in common usage earlier, the first written record to use "California" in reference to the general region north of Mexico dates from 1542, nine years after the southern tip of Baja California first came to the attention of Hernán Cortés. The forbidding terrain of the narrow peninsula, mistakenly believed to be an island for several years, apparently reminded the conquistadors of a place they had read about in the works of a then-popular but now forgotten novel—*The Exploits of Esplandian*—written by Garci Rodriguez de Montalvo around 1500. Esplandian spearheads the resistance at the siege of Constantinople in Montalvo's tale, valiantly protecting the beleaguered Christian city from a horde of pagan marauders. The attackers include one Calafia, Queen of California—a place Montalvo describes as a rugged, rocky island lying on the right hand of the Indies, west of America. It is

MACHO SLUTS

EROTIC FICTION BY PAT CALIFIA

The story of the Amazon queen of California has been well known to scholars and history buffs since the 1860s. "Califia," a variant spelling of the name in Montalvo's 16th-century romance, had become a part of lesbian folklore by the 1970s. In her S/M-oriented essays and fiction, San Francisco writer Pat Califia describes modern-day Amazons every bit as fierce as the ones Montalvo imagined.
Boston: Alyson Publications, 1988.

inhabited by black women warriors with weapons of gold, who ride griffins into battle and feed them on the flesh of conquered men. The imaginary Californians of the story are all too predictably overcome by the pious knights. Their queen converts to Christianity, marries a relative of Esplandian, and eventually returns with him to California. An anxious masculine fantasy about subduing a society of well-armed women: This was the scenario that fueled the Spanish desire to penetrate the "northern mystery" on the margins of their Mexican holdings. One almost begins to wonder if, through some fault line in the fabric of time, the conquistadors somehow caught sight of another Amazonian leader with a name much like Calafia, one who would someday live in our own California amid another fierce female tribe.

The second anecdote involves Walt Whitman. California played a role no less fanciful (and just as queer) in his literary imagination. As the United States thrust its borders westward in 1860 and lurched tragically toward civil war, Whitman published "A Promise to California" in the Calamus cluster of poems in his masterpiece, *Leaves of Grass.* As distinguished literary critic Malcolm Cowley pointed out nearly 50 years ago, the calamus root or "sweet flag" is a large aromatic grass with spears three feet high, native to the Northeast and the Midwest. It served as Whitman's favorite symbol of the phallus, and as the central "leaf of grass" in the poet's greatest work. As Cowley asserted then—and as succeeding generations of gay scholarship have supported—the poems in this section of *Leaves of Grass* address explicitly sexual love between men. The language of "A Promise to California" is ambiguous enough that a general readership would hear only a plea for harmony at a time of unprecedented unrest. Those attuned to Whitman's veiled references, however, understood that he advocated a specifically homoerotic male love as the emotional tie that could best bind the fractious states. Moreover, California represented for Whitman (as it did for many of his fellow citizens) the culmination of the westward-tending process of nation-building, the place where a peculiarly American civilization would one day be realized. In *Democratic Vistas* a decade later, Whitman described his vision of that future:

> Many will say it is a dream, and not follow my inferences; but I confidently expect
> a time when there will be seen, running like a half-hid warp through all the
> myriad audible and visible worldly interests of America, a thread of manly friend-
> ship, fond and loving, pure and sweet, strong and lifelong, carried to degrees
> hitherto unknown—not only giving tone to individual character, and making it

unprecedentedly emotional, muscular, heroic, and refined, but having the deepest relation to general politics. I say democracy infers such loving comradeship as its most inevitable twin or counterpart, without which it would be incomplete, in vain and incapable of perpetuating itself.

Like the conquistadors three centuries before him, Whitman, too, seems to have glimpsed a California not wholly unlike ours today.

The queerness of California was more than a figment of the Euro-American imagination, however, if queerness is considered to be an identity or practice that disrupts normative notions of gender and sexuality. The Catholic priests who accompanied the soldiers during the conquest of North America were both mortified and perplexed by the prevalence of individuals they called by such names as "berdache," "mujerado," "jolla," or "hermaphrodite." These "two-spirit people"

"A Promise to California"

. . . Sojourning Eastward a while
longer, soon I travel toward you, to
remain,
     to teach robust American love,
For I know very well that I and robust
love belong among you, to the
     East and to the West . . .
To the Kanadian of the North, to the
Southerner I love . . .
I believe the main purport of these
States is to found a superb friendship,
exalté, previously unknown,
     Because I perceive it waits, and
has always been waiting, latent in all
men.
             —Walt Whitman,
(lines restored from the manuscript) Calamus
Lovers: Walt Whitman's Working Class Camerados,
edited by Charley Shively (San Francisco: Gay
Sunshine Press, 1987).

*Walt Whitman, frontispiece illustration from
the first edition of* Leaves of Grass *(1855).*
Courtesy of GLHS.

11

"The Father Missionaries of the Mission noticed that among the women (who always worked separately and without mixing with the men) there was one who, by the dress, which was decorously worn, and by the heathen head-dress and ornaments displayed, as well as the manner of working, of sitting, etc., had all the appearances of a woman, but judging by the face and the absence of breasts, though old enough for that, they concluded that he must be a man, so they asked some of the converts. They said that it was a man, but that he passed himself off always for a woman and always went with them and not with the men."

—Father Francisco Palou,
describing a visit to Mission Santa Clara in present-day
San Jose by Chumash Indians in the 18th century.
Quoted by Malcolm Margolin in *The Ohlone Way*
(Berkeley: Heyday Press, 1978), p. 84.

In 1869, the young San Francisco writer Charles Warren Stoddard published "A South Sea Idyl," *a homoerotic short story based on his experiences in Hawaii, in the prominent literary journal* Overland Monthly. *In 1903, he published* For the Pleasure of His Company: An Affair of the Misty City, *an early gay autobiographical novel set in San Francisco.*
Courtesy of San Francisco History Room
(SFHR), San Francisco Public Library
(SFPL).

(the term preferred by most Native Americans today) confounded European beliefs about the proper relationship between anatomy, gender identity, and sexuality, because they had male bodies but lived socially as women and often had intimate physical contact with men. People with female bodies who lived as husbands and warriors also existed in many Native American cultures, but these individuals did not inflame phobic responses to the same extent as their counterparts who transgressed the European norms of sexuality and gender in the other direction. Vilifying male-to-female individuals as sodomites, the mission fathers waged a relentless campaign to eradicate two-spirit traditions throughout the area of Spanish occupation. Although a special two-spirit status was not recognized in all native cultures, male-to-female two-spirit people did have a role among the Ohlone, the principal tribe indigenous to the Bay Area. People with female bodies are not known to have adopted masculine social roles here, although homosexual acts between women seem to have been an unremarkable aspect of conventional feminine sexuality.

It is equally difficult to get a conceptual handle on the history of sexuality in the English-speaking society that took shape in the Bay Area after the Mexican-American war, and after the Gold Rush of 1849 flooded Northern California with tens of thousands of immigrants from the United States. Some of this difficulty is due to the extensive destruction of public records in the great earthquake and fire of 1906. Even those personal accounts that survive, however, are characterized by a Victorian reticence to speak openly of sexual matters—queer or otherwise. More frustrating still for modern scholars who comb the records of the past in search of their sexual ancestors is that contemporary ideas about what it means to be lesbian, gay, bisexual, transgendered, or straight are of startlingly recent origin. Until well into the 20th century, for example, even married men and women tended to spend most of their social lives among members of their own sex. "Homosociality" was the rule rather than the exception, and intense emotional attachments between people of the same sex were quite common. It seems counterintuitive to modern queer sensibilities, but such "passionate friendships" usually did not involve sexual activities—although some such relationships certainly had an erotic aspect. Moreover, even those people who did engage in explicitly homosexual behavior also tended to be involved in heterosexual relationships, making "bisexual" practice—rather than exclusive homosexuality—the norm in queer subcultures. This was especially true for women. Virtual exclusion from the paid work force, coupled with their biological role in reproduction, made it especially difficult for women to completely extricate themselves from the institutions of marriage and the family. Single men, on the other hand, had greater access to new labor markets created by the rapid expansion of industry in the 19th century. They had more geographical mobility, as well as more opportunities to associate with other men in public places. As a result, exclusive homosexuality emerged as a way of life among men earlier than it did for women.

Left and Above: *Vaudevillian Paul Vernon, a San Francisco celebrity in the 1870s.* Courtesy of Bancroft Library, University of California at Berkeley.

"Some nuts."

Kiss me quick.

It's Not What You See but Where and How You Look

These photographs illustrate the difficulties involved in trying to decipher the complexities of our queer past. The pictures {left} of an outing to the beach are from a photo album belonging to a gay man, yet these images contain no content that could be labeled explicitly gay without prior knowledge of the people involved. The pictures above are from an anonymous photo album donated to the Gay and Lesbian Historical Society of Northern California. Because the album includes images of women wearing men's clothes and kissing, the pictures might seem at first glance to represent lesbian lives. However, upon closer examination, the picture of the two women kissing bears a handwritten caption reading "Some Nuts." The women are clearly mugging for the camera. They are more likely to be straight women playing with the boundaries of acceptable behavior. Now notice the expression of the woman in the right margin in the other picture from the same album, as she looks affectionately at another woman (not entirely in frame). The picture is captioned "Kiss Me Quick." In this context, the look takes on an erotic charge; might it be an unspoken acknowledgment of a desire to kiss that cannot be acted upon in the moment? Was the caption added later simply to make fun of the scowl upon the principal subject's face—thus creating a post facto context for the marginal woman's glance that only a subsequent queer viewer would perceive? Or does the context supplied by the caption refer to the circumstances in which the photograph was taken and thus support a definite queer reading of the image? There really is no good way to tell.

Deliberately posed photographs and more formal studio portraiture present the same kinds of interpretive problems as candid snapshots. The couple in theatrical costumes subverts dominant cultural norms of romance by staging them in a manner in which we can see that it is two women playing the lover and the beloved and yet they simultaneously stage heterosexual roles while transgressing their conventions. The two women in sailor suits offer an even more complexly queer sight: an affectionate female couple whose cross-dressing suggests the homoerotic connotations often associated with male sailors. The two photographs of male couples are interesting in that they depict an easy physical affection between men, a comfortable familiarity with other male bodies that has come to be seen as an exclusive characteristic of gay masculinity. But do these images represent gay men or is it that the codes regulating proper expressions of masculinity have changed since the early 20th century? The fact that the pictures on these pages come from postcard collections of self-identified lesbians and gay men indicates that contemporary viewers do see something queer in these images from the past, but there does not seem to be any uncomplicated way to reclaim these photographs as "lesbian" or "gay" representations in the current sense of those words. Photographs courtesy of GLHS.

Woman's Life as Man Told
Wore Male Attire 40 Years

Here is an exclusive picture of **Elvira Mugarrietta,** who for 40 years masqueraded as a man under the name of Jack Bee Garland because skirts barred her from the life she wanted to lead. This photograph was taken in 1898, in Stockton.

Your last letter, short, but very nice and dated God knows when reached me this afternoon and here I am writing to you again. You will say to yourself "What is the matter with the old boy out in California? He has doubtless gone crazy."

And you will be dam right. He has. Over women at that. To be exact, over one woman . . . One who cries all the time and who won't eat when you tell her to. I have got her in a hospital locked up although her health is perfect and I am trying to turn her over to her sister who also cries all the time and who wants her very much. But she won't go to her sister or to any other reasonable place. All she wants is the boys clothes that she has been wearing for more than ten years.

I have told you of this girl before and of her strange life which is, in truth, stranger than any tale the fiction writers have ever put upon paper . . . This girl, not at all mannish, the gently raised daughter of a general in the old regular army of Mexico, changed in an hour to a smart swaggering boasting young man, and successfully maintained that character for fifteen or more years, serving one enlistment in our regular army, only to be caught a few weeks ago by the Los Angeles police while acting as a secretary in a branch of the Young Men's Christian Association.

If that tale doesn't beat anything ever invented I'll give up.

She would not have been caught at this time were it not that, disregarding notices posted, she went for a walk out on the dock at San Pedro, and was arrested on suspicion of being a German spy and her long deception discovered. When her room was searched

The picture of pre–World War II sexuality becomes more complex the more one pays attention to gender. Earlier generations of queer people—as well as the straight doctors, psychiatrists, social scientists, and legal experts who studied them—typically considered same-sex activity to involve a gender inversion for one of the partners. It was the "fairies," "pansies," "butches," and "bulldaggers" who served as the visible and vocal emblems of queer life before the mid-20th century, while the conventionally gendered "normal" men and "femme" women who chose they found (this is silly to confess) my picture under her pillow. It was one of those old attorney general pictures from the last campaign and the infernal thing had my name in big black letters printed under it . . .

She called herself "Ben Garland the Soldier-Poet" and actually sold stuff which was published in the "Sunday Chronicle."

She refused to tell the Los Angeles officers anything about herself so the court with my picture as a clue sent her up here and sent the officer who brought her after me. We locked her up at St. Lukes and I sent for her sister, a fine and faithful woman, the wife of a very well known wealthy man of this city. She accounted for my picture by telling the Los Angeles judge that I was "a gentleman who had been kind to her when she was in difficulties."

Up to the present she has flatly refused to go back to her own sex and flatly says that she would rather go to prison than do so. Hunger strikes are a favorite pastime with her and when they have been persisted in for over one day I am sent for to coax her to eat. When I arrive and begin coaxing she begins to weep and continues until I leave but when I am gone she takes food "to keep the doctors from annoying me." Our present scheme to get her started upon rational lines consists in me telling her to dry her tears and affect to submit to her sister; to put on petticoats for a while and when everything had blown over and all was quiet she could make another "sneak." I put this scheme to her this evening and she listened attentively and we think it is going to work. She asked me if I would permit myself to go traipsing around in corset and skirts. I told her I was sure I would make a sensation in apparel of that kind [but] that I would willingly do it if thereby I might gain my liberty. I told her that I would go so far as to wear my hair dutch cut with great ribbons in it and would don pinafores and roll a hoop through the park rather than stay locked up in a smelly hospital. . . To get back to Ben Garland, the soldier-poet, nobody can tell how the muddle "it" has got itself into is going to end. While to an onlooker it is extremely ludicrous, to her and especially to the sister it approaches pretty near to being a tragedy.

"inverts" as their partners are the curiously silent figures. Cross-gender expression was not confined to gay drag, butch lesbian, or heterosexual transvestite subcultures in the late 19th and early 20th centuries, however. Rather, it was an unremarkable feature in many parades, costume balls, vaudeville routines, and college skits. It might be part of Sunday afternoon socializing with friends and family—especially if somebody had a camera, and an uncle or nephew was visiting with his new army uniform for nieces or aunts to try on. And rather than

Monwell Boyfrank, an early 20th-century cowboy who later moved to California and became a sailor, reminisced about how partnerships with other men, encouraged by the trail boss, often eventually became sexual: "At first pairing they'd solace each other gingerly and, as bashfulness waned, manually. As trust in mutual good will matured, they'd graduate to the ecstatically comforting 69 . . . Folk know not how cock-hungry men get. . . [Attraction for another cowboy] was at first rooted in admiration, infatuation, a sensed need of an ally, loneliness and yearning, but it regularly ripened into love."

Quoted by Walter Williams in
Spirit and the Flesh: Sexual Diversity in American Indian Culture
(Boston: Beacon Press, 1986), p. 159.

February 1931.

Magnus Hirschfeld, a leader of the homosexual emancipation movement in Germany, visited San Francisco during a world tour. In "Hypocrisy in U.S. Flayed by Dr. Hirschfeld," a February 25, 1931, *San Francisco Examiner* interview, the eminent sexologist criticized laws against alcohol, sex between unmarried partners, and birth control.

Right: *Deaf sculptor Douglas Tilden's "Mechanics Monument" (1894) celebrates working-class male youth, beauty, and homosocial bonding. The homoerotic overtones in this bronze sculpture, as well in other works such as "The Football Players" at the University of California at Berkeley and "Spanish-American Volunteers" on Market Street, support the idea that Tilden may have been gay. His wife divorced him on grounds of "desertion," and his principal patron was James Phelan—San Francisco mayor, U.S. senator, and (in the circumspect wording of society historian Julia Altrocchi) "an unimpeachable bachelor." After living and working for many years in Paris and gaining a reputation in Europe as part of the Beaux Arts school, Tilden died at his Berkeley studio in 1935 alone, impoverished, and critically neglected.* Courtesy of SFHR, SFPL.

being considered somewhat tawdry adult fare, female impersonation was part of the legitimate theater, and was considered perfectly acceptable family entertainment (much as racial impersonation in minstrel shows was viewed by white audiences as perfectly unobjectionable).

In spite of the fact that social conditions in the Bay Area during the hundred years before World War II would seem to have been especially conducive to homosexual activity, remarkably little documentation of queer sexuality has turned up—and those records that have come to light are almost certainly not representative of the spectrum of possibilities that existed then. Much of what is known about queer history in this period is due to the arrest of male prostitutes in feminine attire, or of females discovered to be living as men. And yet opportunities for other types of queer behavior abounded. Because of the Gold Rush, the population of San Francisco was roughly 90 percent male throughout the 1850s and remained disproportionately high for years afterward. Historical research in other regions has shown that homosexual activity was common in such predominantly male societies—especially among men who worked in occupations that typically involved long absences from women or that took them to isolated geographical locations. Well-developed male homosexual subcultures have been documented among pirates, sailors, and cowboys—and while there are only slim clues to verify that such a lifestyle existed in the Bay Area in the mid-19th century, there is also no reason to suspect that the men here departed from this general sociological pattern. There are apocryphal tales of all-male square dances, where the man dancing the woman's part wore a red bandanna on his arm—the precursor of the modern hanky code according to contemporary gay folklore. And activities in the Barbary Coast, old San Francisco's infamous saloon and brothel district, earned the city one of its earliest nicknames—Sodom by the Sea. Whatever sexual demimonde existed here was so beyond the realm of public discussion, however, that even Oscar Wilde, the era's most celebrated libertine, made no mention of it when he visited San Francisco in 1882.

Between the 1890s and 1920s, however, faint but recognizable traces of modern sexual identities and communities began to appear. One individual who served as a case study in German sexologist Magnus Hirschfeld's pioneering 1910 study of transgendered people described living as a woman in San Francisco in the 1890s and working as a cook, seamstress, and housekeeper for actresses in the city's theater district. In 1896, local resident Robert Allan Nicol wrote to Edward Carpenter, the British champion of homosexual emancipation, that "really you have quite a following in San Francisco alone." Edward Stevenson described the prevalence of male prostitution among troops stationed at the Presidio during the Spanish-American War of 1898 in his somewhat eccentric 1908 treatise *The Intersexes: A History of Similisexualism as a Problem in Social Life*. In 1903, San Franciscan Charles Warren Stoddard published *For the Pleasure of His Company: An Affair of the Misty City*, his semi-autobiographical novel depicting a life of gay middle-class respectability. If "slumming" was as popular a middle-class pastime in the Bay Area as it was in New York during this period, men like those described by Stoddard may well have frequented the Dash, San Francisco's earliest known gay bar, located at 574 Pacific Street. The saloon and dance hall, which featured female impersonators, was shut down by city officials in 1908.

Gertrude Stein and Alice B. Toklas—still perhaps the most renowned lesbian couple in the English-speaking world—both grew up in the Bay Area before the turn of the century. Stein had moved at age five with her family to Oakland, where her father was vice-president of the Omnibus Cable Company. After being orphaned in 1891, she lived for a few years with an older brother in San Francisco before attending college on the East Coast. Stein moved permanently to Paris in 1903 and became part of a circle of remarkably talented writers and artists, including then-unknown Pablo Picasso. When Stein's brother and sister-in-law (who had also relocated to Paris) went home after the 1906 San Francisco Earthquake to assess the damage to their real estate holdings, they brought with them the first Modernist avant-garde paintings ever seen in the United States. The Steins exhibited recent work by their friend Henri Matisse for San Francisco's intellectual elites, and one of those who came to see this provocative new style of painting was

Alexander Berkman, an anarchist associate of Emma Goldman, gave a public speech, "Homosexuality and Sex Life in Prison," attended by a large crowd in San Francisco in June 1915. Courtesy of SFHR, SFPL.

"Homosexuality—A Military Menace," one of the earliest medical articles on how to recognize homosexuals in the U.S. armed forces, was published by Dr. Albert Abrams in San Francisco in 1918.

19

20

Left: *Alice B. Toklas was born in San Francisco on April 30, 1877, and moved to Paris in 1906. She returned to San Francisco in 1935, staying at the Mark Hopkins Hotel with Gertrude Stein. While having her hair cut in an 18th-century French style, Alice remarked, "Just the old men wear it that way now, but hair must be short. San Francisco is a good town for haircuts."* Courtesy of Bancroft Library, University of California at Berkeley.

Opposite Page: *In 1935, Gertrude Stein (third from the left) returned to East Oakland to see the house at 13th Avenue and 25th Street to which her family had moved in 1879. When she saw that the house where she had lived was gone and had been built over with little houses, she observed that there was "no there there." Her poignant comment has been repeatedly misinterpreted as dismissive of the city of Oakland.* Courtesy of Bancroft Library, University of California at Berkeley.

a 28-year-old woman, Alice Toklas. Toklas had inherited a modest fortune from her grandfather's gold mines on Mokulumne Hill in the San Joaquin Valley, and she was not optimistic about her hometown's prospects in the aftermath of the recent catastrophe. She liked the world she glimpsed through Matisse's canvases, and accordingly set off for France with her friend Harriet Levy. Levy was a friend of the Stein family, and introduced Alice to Gertrude the moment they arrived in Paris. The relationship that began that day endured until Stein's death in 1946. The couple returned to the Bay Area only once, in 1935, on a speaking tour after Stein had won international fame as leading light of Modernist literature.

☾

The Bay Area supported another remarkable woman who surrounded herself with an impressive circle of intellectual and literary talent. The poet Elsa Gidlow, whose 1923 volume *On a Grey Thread* was likely the first book of explicitly lesbian poetry published in North America, moved to San Fancisco in 1926

Elsa Gidlow

Poet Elsa Gidlow, pictured here as a young woman, lived for many years in Marin County. Throughout her life, she attracted a circle of remarkable women, including her lover, Isabelle Quallo. Photographs courtesy of GLHS, Elsa Gidlow Collection.

Opposite Page: *Druid Heights, Gidlow's home.* Photograph by Marcellina Martin, 1985.

Elsa Gidlow

Isabelle Quallo, Gidlow's lover.

Margaret Chung, friend of Elsa Gidlow

and supported herself primarily by editing and publishing a variety of small newsletters and trade publications. She befriended the likes of Robinson and Una Jeffers and Kenneth Rexroth, and soon became a fixture in the city's radical and bohemian subcultures. Gidlow purchased "Madrona," a rustic Marin County retreat, in 1940. "Druid Heights," near Mill Valley, to which she relocated in 1954, became a spiritual home to a number of influential thinkers and writers, including prostitution rights activist Margo St. James and Alan Watts, who helped popularize Buddhist philosophy in the United States.

Environments such as the one Gidlow built up around herself—private spaces in which queer people and their friends could socialize and build personal

networks—had been especially important during Prohibition, when federal laws against the production and consumption of alcohol drove bars underground. After the repeal of Prohibition, a number of gay bars quickly sprang up, the first of which was Finocchio's. From the moment it surreptitiously opened its doors as a speakeasy in 1929 until the present day, Finocchio's main attraction has been female impersonation. Although it has always been a tourist bar, Finocchio's served a significantly gay and lesbian clientele for decades. After becoming a legal establishment in 1933, Finocchio's catered to the brief "pansy craze" that swept the nation in the early 1930s (similar in many ways to the mainstream fascination with cross-dressing in the 1990s). The club was soon part of an established circuit of gay bohemian nightspots in North Beach frequented by the literary crowd. Other bars on the circuit included Mona's—the city's first lesbian establishment— and the legendary Black Cat Cafe, which would become an icon of San Francisco bohemian culture in the postwar years.

Bars in different parts of the city drew different kinds of crowds. The Sailor Boy Tavern, established in 1938 on Howard Street a block away from the Embarcadero YMCA, had a rougher clientele than the Fireside, a quiet restaurant and bar that opened on California Street in 1937. The Old Crow, which had been

San Francisco's notorious Barbary Coast circa the 1920s. The first known gay bar in the vicinity dates from 1908, but by then the district had already helped earn the city its 19th-century nickname, "Sodom by the Sea." By the 1930s, what had been the Barbary Coast supported such celebrated gay nightspots as Finocchio's, Mona's, and the Black Cat Cafe. Courtesy of SFHR, SFPL.

on Market Street since 1935, was the oldest gay bar in San Francisco when it closed in 1980. It attracted relatively mature and settled men as patrons and had a rigorously enforced policy of excluding all women. The White Horse in Berkeley has been drawing a noticeably gay mixed clientele since 1933 and is the oldest continuously operating gay bar in the Bay Area.

Bars were not the only sites for gay public sociability in the 1930s—Jack's Turkish Baths and the Third Street Baths both opened in this decade, and public restrooms had long since become places where gay men looked for "tearoom trade." Lou Rand Hogan, the gay gourmet chef who later achieved modest fame with his food columns and cookbooks, knew of no gay bars as such when he first became sexually active in San Francisco in the 1920s—cruising Market Street near the waterfront was how most men he knew met their partners.

It is also important to recognize that the racial segregation of many public places made bar culture more important for white lesbians and gays than it did for African Americans and other people of color. The first black-owned and oriented gay bar in the city, the Big Glass on Fillmore, did not open until 1964. Social his-

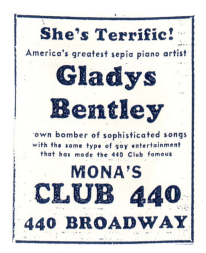

She's Terrific!
America's greatest sepia piano artist
Gladys Bentley
·own bomber of sophisticated songs
with the same type of gay entertainment
that has made the 440 Club famous
MONA'S
CLUB 440
440 BROADWAY

AMERICAS'
MOST UNUSUAL
NIGHT CLUB
FINOCCHIO

Top Left and Right: *Mona's: Gladys Bentley*
Above: *Finocchio's*
Right: *Black Cat Cafe*

The Black Cat Cafe
"Bohemia of the Barbary Coast"

710 Montgomery Street
San Francisco, Calif.
Telephone SUtter 1-9501

"PREJUDICE AGAINST HOMOSEXU-ALS—In Berkeley a fortnight ago, a group of young men entertained themselves. Some wore female attire; some danced and talked as women do. All acted naturally and without restraint. They enjoyed the occasion and returned to their homes, their loved ones, or their work. This ordinary occurrence in the lives of human beings still afforded child-minded members of the community much amusement. Men and women, apparently intelligent and kind, are using the incident as subject for parlor conversation, referring to the young men as though they were visitors to the earth from some strange and unknown land. Perhaps these normal people do not know EVERY MAN AND WOMAN IS POTENTIALLY HOMOSEXUAL."

San Francisco Spokesman,
November 3, 1932.
This African American newspaper reveals
how social mores about sexuality
sometimes varied
in different ethnic communities.

Harry Hay, founder of the Mattachine Society in the 1950s, moved in gay theater and artistic circles in San Francisco during the 1930s, when he was an openly gay Stanford undergraduate. Courtesy of Stuart Timmons.

torians are beginning to realize that the bar culture's sojourn into the criminal underworld during Prohibition had important consequences that helped shape contemporary queer life. Many middle-class white people first encountered a countercultural lifestyle in the illegal speakeasies, and first mixed socially with people from different economic and ethnic backgrounds. The Prohibition years left traces in queer argot as well. "Straight" referred primarily to law-abiding citizens before the 1930s—and criminals, rather than gays, were said to be "in the life."

As the financial crisis of the late 1920s deepened into a devastating economic depression, lesbians and gays already cynical about futile government attempts to regulate their private lives found it increasingly easy to question the legitimacy of the established social order. Many trends of the tumultuous Depression decade were exemplified in the life of Harry Hay, a young student at Stanford in 1930–32. Hay used his rather effeminate manner to attract the attention of other gay college men, but he soon grew frustrated with the clandestine lifestyle he had to adopt in Palo Alto; he quickly found himself spending most of his social time in San Francisco's theatrical and artistic circles and frequenting an invitation-only speakeasy predominantly patronized by gay clients. Hay left Stanford altogether in 1932, after being ostracized by the campus community following his virtually unprecedented decision to publicly declare his homosexuality. Hay moved to Hollywood to work in the film industry and fell in with a politically radical crowd. He returned to the Bay Area briefly in 1934 with his political mentor, the actor Will Geer, to participate in the massive San Francisco General Strike. That event changed Hay's life—and the course of homosexual politics in the United States. Hay recalled years later that after witnessing the governor send in state militia troops to fire on striking maritime labor union members, hearing bullets zing past his ears, and watching the massive funeral procession for the slain workers surge down Market Street, he was caught by "the siren song of Revolution." A Communist Party member for much of the 1930s (and beyond), Hay was distressed by the Left's official homophobia, but it was through his radical work that Hay first began to consider forming a homosexual political organization. That vision was not realized until after World War II, when Hay helped establish the Mattachine Society in Los Angeles, but it was in the streets of San Francisco during some of the darkest days of the Great Depression that the first enduring gay rights group began to take shape in its founder's consciousness.

The San Francisco General Strike of 1933 was perhaps the most dramatic instance of organized labor protest during the Great Depression, bringing the city to a standstill until state militia troops fired on striking workers. Harry Hay, who later organized the first nationwide gay rights group, credits the San Francisco General Strike with radicalizing him. Courtesy of SFHR, SFPL.

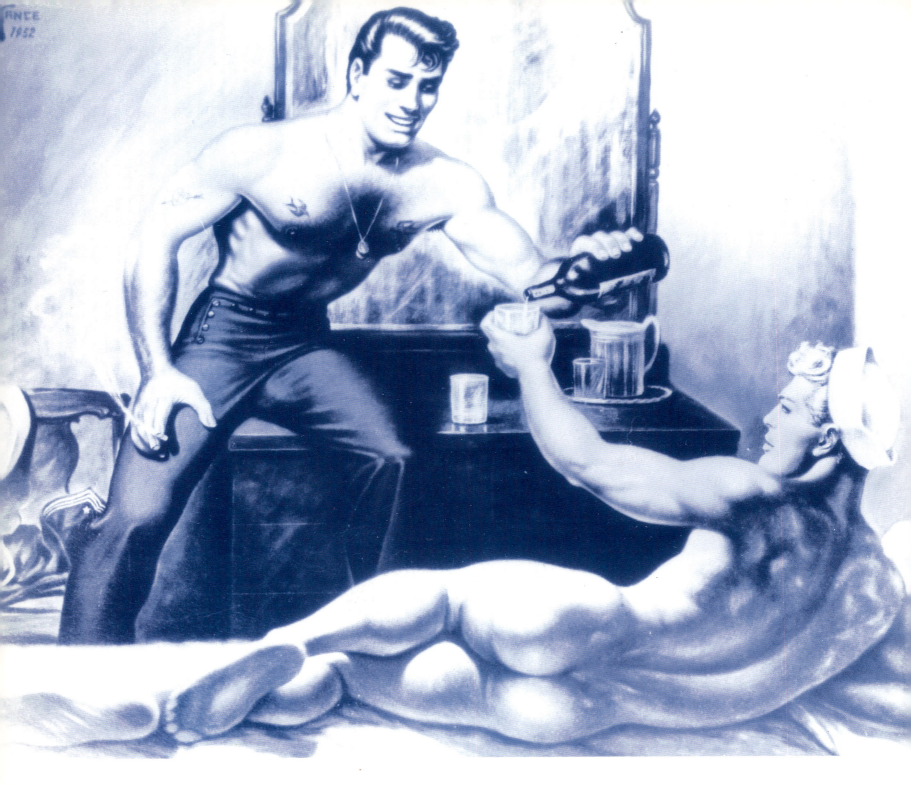

Sailors, said to be the most available of men in uniforms, were plentiful in San Francisco as they shipped in and out of Bay Area naval bases. In Shore Leave *(1952), homoerotic artist George Quaintance depicts a quintessential wartime liaison.* Courtesy GLHS.

From War to Revolution, 1940–1967

World War II was a transformative event in the history of modern queer communities and identities. It not only changed the personal lives of countless thousands of individual men and women, it also shifted the role of sexuality in American public life and altered the social geography of urban centers like San Francisco. Like the Gold Rush a hundred years earlier, World War II drew masses of people out of their accustomed walks of life and threw them together in sex-segregated settings, into situations where the normal rules of social interaction were often disregarded. Many people who had felt same-sex desires—but who never knew there were other people like themselves—had their first homosexual encounters as a direct result of their military service or their participation in the wartime labor market. World War II was also the first time the military actively sought to ferret out gay and lesbian service members and to dishonorably discharge them solely on the basis of their sexuality. As one of the primary departure points for troops headed to the Pacific theater, San Francisco's wartime population swelled with government-certified

During World War II, Treasure Island Naval Hospital psychiatric ward functioned as a holding pen for sailors about to be discharged from military service because of their sexual orientation. Psychiatrists conducted extensive interviews with gay men to try to discover the causes of homosexuality. After the war, Dr. Karl M. Bowman (pictured above) and Bernice Engle of the Langley Porter Clinic in San Francisco published "The Problem of Homosexuality," one of a number of reports released during the 1950s and 1960s that drew on wartime research on human sexuality and discussed the effects of castration, lobotomy, electroshock, and other forms of "treatment" for homosexuals.
Courtesy of SFHR, SFPL.

homosexuals—many of whom were none too anxious to return to their hometowns and only too eager to remain in the Bay Area.

The number of gay bars and restaurants in the city burgeoned along with its wartime population. Military personnel searching for such establishments received an inadvertent boost from the armed services themselves—lists of off-limits bars were routinely posted on military bases. Gay soldiers and sailors needed only to check the list and slip into their civvies before heading out for an illicit night on the town. Sexual activity was so rampant that the navy launched an investigation into the dramatic rise in venereal disease rates among naval personnel in the Bay Area, Congress conducted hearings on moral conditions in nearby army camps, and a California State Assembly committee began looking into lax enforcement of liquor laws in San Francisco. A serious anti-vice crackdown was underway by the summer of 1942, resulting in the closure of dozens of bars and eateries, as well as increased surveillance of cruising grounds like Union Square. Because nightspots that attracted a noticeably "swishy" crowd were likely targets for raids, many gays—especially officers—preferred to spend their after-duty hours in well-heeled establishments like the Top of the Mark in the posh Mark Hopkins Hotel, where a discreet gay clientele mingled fluidly with the predominantly straight crowd.

Homosexuality attained a new level of public notoriety as a result of the war, and right-wing politicians like Joseph McCarthy and Californian Richard Nixon viewed it as a significant social problem in the immediate post war years, a threat to their "American Way of Life" on a par with international communist conspiracies. As community institutions of unparalleled importance in an era before any political or social organizations existed for lesbians and gay men, bars bore the brunt of this stepped-up anti-gay activity. The state Alcoholic Beverage Commission (ABC), which had the power to revoke liquor licenses, was the primary bureaucratic body that attempted to regulate queer sociability by policing gay bars and taverns. Because homosexuality was by definition illegal, throughout the 1940s bars could be closed simply because they served drinks to self-professed homosexuals in the presence of undercover ABC officers. A landmark California Supreme Court case overturned this practice in 1951—due largely to the efforts of Sol Stoumen, the straight owner of the Black Cat Cafe, who took a principled stand in favor of freedom of assembly for all his customers. As a result of this victory, however, San Francisco police and the ABC began a punitive campaign against gay bars

HOMOS INVADE S.F.

The Truth

VOL. 1, No. 2   MONDAY, JULY 11, 1949, SAN FRANCISCO, CALIF.   62

I Was A Racket Girl

★ ★ ★ ★ ★

A NEW SERIES OF ARTICLES PORTRAYING THE
LIFE OF A GIRL WHO LIVED BY HER WITS . . . .

By JEANNE
(As told to Rods Worth)

I was a racket girl.

Yes, I was a racket girl, but now as I look back on those muddled years—it all seems like a bad dream.

My four years of disorder as a depraved delinquent are now of the past.

My four years as a racket girl is now a closed chapter in my life—

Perversion Accompanies Strange Characters As Citizens Fear Rights Loss

San Francisco is rapidly becoming the central gathering-point of lesbians and homo-sexuals in California. This city is taking away this unwanted laurels from Los Angeles without a fight. The sappy tolerance of San Francisco is nowhere more apparent than in the green light that we have given to the assorted bunch of lesbians and homos to practice their quirks in our fair city.

"San Francisco is rapidly becoming the central gathering point of lesbians and homosexuals in California. This city is taking away {these} unwanted laurels from Los Angeles without a fight. The sappy tolerance of San Francisco is nowhere more apparent than in the green light that we have given to the assorted bunch of lesbians and homos to practice their quirks in our fair city."
—The Truth, July 11, 1949.

that flared intermittently for more than a decade, produced three other important state supreme court rulings, and culminated in the eventual closure of the Black Cat in 1963.

Bohemian and gay bar culture, particularly in the North Beach neighborhood, overlapped with the Beat literary movement, some of whose most celebrated representatives were gay and bisexual men. In 1955, Allen Ginsberg's "Howl" electrified San Francisco audiences with its audacious images of gay sexuality. The poem catapulted Ginsberg and the Beat Generation to lasting fame two years later when San Francisco Police Captain William Hanrahan confiscated copies of *Howl and Other Poems* from City Lights Bookstore and arrested owner Lawrence Ferlinghetti on obscenity charges. The charges were subsequently overturned, but not before the incident had become a cause célèbre among civil libertarians across the country. Ginsberg and such companions as Jack Kerouac and Neal Cassady frequented San Francisco as part of the travel circuit described in Kerouac's quintessential Beat novel *On the Road,* and thus became associated with the city's bohemian reputation. None of the principal Beat figures maintained a long-term presence here, however.

Below: Gay Bar, *by Helen P. Branson, offers an insider's view of the environment that nurtured important elements of our contemporary queer culture in the years following World War II.* Courtesy of GLHS.

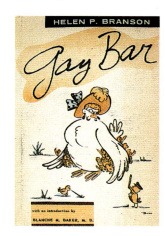

HELEN P. BRANSON

Gay Bar

with an introduction by
BLANCHE M. BAKER, M. D.

31

"Yes, thinking back, it was glorious. To hell with your modern 'gay' bars (which aren't . . .); the mad, modern cruising (but where . . . ?); the 'anything goes' Baths (where there are no REAL men, and who wants cat meat . . . ?). And as for the Beaches and Parks, who really wants sand, or fox-tails, in her snatch? Yes, 'twas better back then, when there were MEN? Men who treated a 'girl' like a lady. And paid for it. Bought their own booze, and appreciated the service. A 'trick' was for a whole weekend, or 48 hours, or longer. Many even lasted out the year, possibly the next, too. And, you stayed at home, and cooked and drank a little, and loved, and lived! Nowadays, it's to the Baths for 6 quick "ki-ki" numbers with other fags; or under the Pier for a couple, and then a third who turns out to be the Law. And so on . . ."

—Lou Rand Hogan,
whose reminiscences of Los Angeles and San Francisco from the 1920s to the 1940s appeared as a six-part series entitled "The Golden Age of the Queens" in the *Bay Area Reporter* under the byline "Toto le Grand" in September 1974.

1940s drag queens.

Another coterie of artists and writers sometimes considered part of a broadly defined Beat sensibility had more indigenous roots in the Bay Area. The poet Robert Duncan, born in Oakland and schooled at UC Berkeley, first achieved national notoriety with the 1944 publication of "The Homosexual in Society," one of the earliest public declarations of homosexual identity and a spirited defense of homosexual civil rights. Although Duncan harshly criticized the tendency to celebrate queer cultural differences from mainstream society (a tendency that he felt robbed queer people of their full humanity), his essay is significant for its characterization of homosexuals as members of a politically oppressed minority, similar to Jews and blacks. While attending college in the immediate postwar years, Duncan was part of the self-styled "Berkeley Renaissance." This literary circle, which later included Duncan's lover Jess Collins, initially consisted of Robin Blaser and the anarchistic Jack Spicer, whose elegiac imagery made frequent reference to the Bay Area's bohemian, gay, and politically radical subcultures. Another local figure, Modesto-born filmmaker and writer James Broughton, also achieved national attention in the postwar years. Self-described as a "pansexual androgyne,"

Excerpts from 1949 California State Penal Code:

"a. In general: The law approves and recognizes only one method of sexual intercourse. That method is the relationship between the sex organ of a man and the sex organ of a woman. Other practices of sexual gratification such as connections per anus or per os (mouth) are forbidden. These other practices are here classed as 'unnatural' in the sense that they are proscribed by law.

"b. *Relations Between Man and Man*

"(1) Sodomy is copulation between the male organ and the anus of the other party. Sexual intercourse between males per anus has been practiced at least as far back as Biblical times in the town of Sodom; whence comes the term. The term sodomy has come to have a much broader meaning than this in a number of states and even covers most of the crimes listed below as 'unnatural practices.'

"Sodomy, in its narrow and historical sense, is a crime for either party in California under Penal Code Section 286.

"c. *Relations Between Man and Woman*

"It is no defense to any of these crimes [sodomy, fellatio, cunnilingus] that the parties are married to each other. Thus in spite of discussion in medical or other treatises on marital relationships, these practices are illegal in every state.

"These crimes are felonies in California and the maximum penalties are 20 years for sodomy and 16 years for fellatio or cunnilingus . . .

"d. *Relations Between Woman and Woman*

"If cunnilingus, the oral copulation of the female sex organs, is practiced by a woman it is a crime in California for both parties under Penal Code Section 288a."

When I praise the sun or any bronze god derived from it/Don't think I wouldn't rather praise the very tall blond boy/Who ate all of my potato-chips at the Red Lizard/It's just that I won't see him when I open my eyes/And I will see the sun.
—Jack Spicer,
"Imaginary Elegies," 1945. In *New American Poetry, 1945–1960*, ed. Donald Allen, (New York: Grove Press, 1960).

"There is in the modern scene no homosexual who has been willing to take in his own persecution a battlefront toward human freedom. Almost coincident with the first declarations for homosexual rights was the growth of a cult of homosexual superiority to the human race, the cultivation of a secret language, the *camp,* a tone and a vocabulary that is loaded with contempt for the human . . . [O]nly one devotion can be held by a human being [committed to] a creative life and expression, and that is a devotion to human freedom, toward the liberation of human love, human conflicts, human aspirations. To do this one must disown *all* the special groups (nations, religions, sexes, races) that would claim allegience . . . It must always be remembered that one's own honesty, one's battle against the inhumanity of his own group (be it against patriotism, against bigotry, against, in this specific case, the homosexual cult) is not a battle that can be won in the immediate scene. The forces of inhumanity are overwhelming, but only one's continued opposition can make any other order possible."

—San Francisco poet
Robert Duncan,
"The Homosexual in Society," *Politics,*
August 1944.

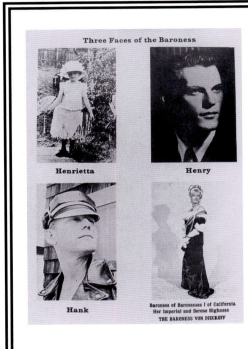

Three Faces of the Baroness

Henrietta

Henry

Hank

Baroness of Baronesses I of California
Her Imperial and Serene Highness
THE BARONESS VON DIECKOFF

"BAGADRAG BY THE BAY,
August 1948
        Lake Temescal in the Berkeley Hills has become the favorite place for many members of the San Francisco social set. Most any day one can see the creme de la creme sunning themselves over there. Mrs. Buttin-Harman and her chum Baroness Nelson von Dieckoff (who has been estranged from her socialite husband since January of this year) have both acquired BEAUTIFUL tans. This pair of blonde beauties have been the reigning queens of the lake this summer."
Henry Dieckoff Papers, GLHS.

Broughton was involved with the experimental Art in Cinema film group at the San Francisco Museum of Modern Art, wrote for the Playhouse Repertory Theater, and taught at the San Francisco Art Institute.

Many lesbians and gays who felt shunted to the margins of society found in the Beat subculture and its associated artistic tendencies a positive and empowering celebration of an "outsider" status with which they could easily identify. The Beats, however, represented only one of many queer cultural styles in the Bay Area. Their dead-serious hypermasculinity was fundamentally at odds with the campy humor of the male drag culture, for example, and had little room, if any, for lesbian participation. Indeed, it is somewhat anachronistic to speak of a lesbian *and* gay community at this time. Although queer men and women sometimes frequented the same bohemian bars, lesbian and gay subcultures diverged more often than they intersected. Court cases in the 1950s would increasingly define lesbianism and male gayness as twin aspects of a generalized homosexual condition —and thus help bring about the very identities they described—but sociologically, gay men and lesbians were often worlds apart. Quite independently of men, women who had sex with other women had their own social networks, their own "butch/femme" styles of gender presentation, and their own bars. The Tin Angel, 12 Adler, and Tommy's Place were all known for their lesbian clientele in the 1950s.

While homosexuality had become more visible in the decades following World War II than in the decades preceding it, most people who had same-sex desires or gender-transgressive appearances still found it difficult to locate others who shared their proclivities. Although the bars served as the principal means of entering queer cultural space or forming a queer personal identity, other avenues were also available. Lesbian "pulp" novels—cheaply produced paperbacks aimed primarily at a male audience titillated by the thought of two women having sex—awakened many budding lesbian sensibilities. Although most of these novels were written by men and straight women (including several by science fiction writer Marion Zimmer Bradley), some of the authors were indeed lesbians themselves and tried to work within the conventions of the sensationalistic pulp genre to infuse their books with a truly informed queer point of view. Physique and body-building magazines functioned similarly for gay men by providing images intended for straight audiences that could be appropriated by queer readers. In a time before the widespread availability of gay and lesbian self-representation, such images and text supplied the bulk of material for queer erotic fantasies.

One of the most distinctive features of the Bay Area's queer cultural landscape during the 1950s was the emergence of the so-called homophile organizations. Shaped partly in reaction to the virulent homophobia of McCarthyism, these assimilationist Cold War–era groups primarily sought to educate the general pub-

Left: *"I remember one time I went to San Francisco with a couple other friends I had met. They were gay and it was really nice for me . . . It was a private house that they had rented, or a basement or something. When we got there they had all these women that were dressed up in men's clothes. And I had never seen that before . . . and I was just fascinated. So every time they had a party in San Francisco I was ready to go!. . . San Francisco had lots of parties at that time . . . This group that I was acquainted with really didn't go to gay bars. They would just have one house party after another . . . Sometimes you had to pay a cover to go in, sometimes you didn't. You'd bring your own drinks if you wanted to, or else they would sell you drinks, stuff like that. They'd make a big pot of spaghetti or chili or something. And then all you would do would be to dance . . . In San Francisco I don't ever recall a bar that had a majority of the women that were black. The majority of women were always white . . . I can't remember their names but there were just lots of bars and you could just have a good time dancing and stuff. But in the bars there was {mostly} one color and not the other. We all got along, but the house parties were mainly black. There were a few Caucasians, but not a lot, just a few."*

—Wilma Johnson (pseud.),
describing the primarily African American house-
party circuit in San Francisco in the early 1960s.
Oral history interview courtesy of Nan Alamilla
Boyd and the Oral History Project of the GLHS.

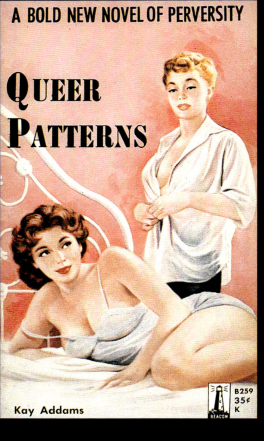

A BOLD NEW NOVEL OF PERVERSITY

Queer Patterns

Kay Addams

B259
35¢
K

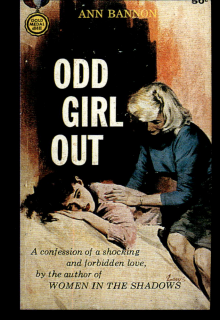

ANN BANNON

ODD GIRL OUT

*A confession of a shocking
and forbidden love,
by the author of*
WOMEN IN THE SHADOWS

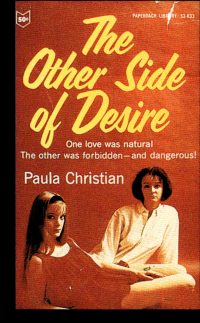

The Other Side of Desire

One love was natural
The other was forbidden—and dangerous!

Paula Christian

Left: *Queer Patterns.*
Courtesy of Gay/Lesbian Center (GLC), SFPL.
Above Left: *Odd Girl Out.*
Ann Bannon of Sacramento penned Odd Girl
Out, *one of many popular lesbian pulp novels
that were often set in Greenwich Village or
Hollywood.* Courtesy of GLC, SFPL.
Above Right: *The Other Side of Desire.*
Courtesy of Susan Stryker.
Right: *Lesbian Web of Evil.*
Courtesy of GLC, SFPL.

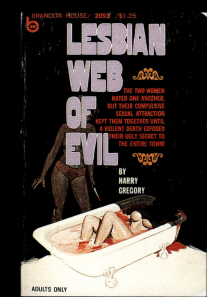

BRANDON HOUSE/ 2093 /$1.25

LESBIAN WEB OF EVIL

THE TWO WOMEN
HATED ONE ANOTHER,
BUT THEIR COMPULSIVE
SEXUAL ATTRACTION
KEPT THEM TOGETHER UNTIL
A VIOLENT DEATH EXPOSED
THEIR UGLY SECRET TO
THE ENTIRE TOWN!

BY
HARRY
GREGORY

ADULTS ONLY

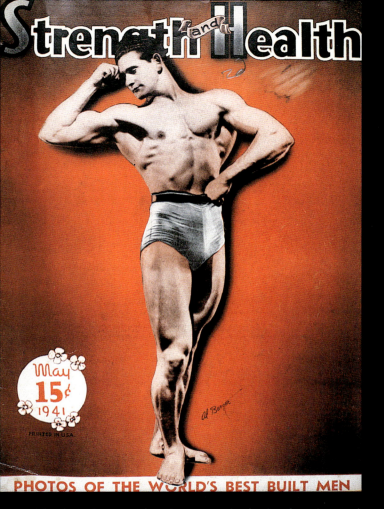

Above: *Though aimed at a straight audience, gay readers found much to admire in physique magazines such as* Strength and Health. Courtesy of GLHS.

The Gay Detective (Sabre, 1961), considered one of the first gay detective novels, was written by Lou Rand Hogan. Rewritten and published as Rough Trade, *the novel is set in "Bay City," so obviously modeled on San Francisco that it is easy to spot local people and places.*

Gay Detective. Courtesy of GLC, SFPL.

Rough Trade. Courtesy of GLC, SFPL.

I LEFT MY HEART
IN SAN FRANCISCO

MUSIC BY
GEORGE CORY
WORDS BY
DOUGLASS CROSS

Recorded by
TONY BENNETT
on Columbia Records

85¢

SHEET MUSIC INSTITUTE
10014

GENERAL MUSIC PUBLISHING COMPANY, INC.

In 1954, Douglass Cross and his lover George Cory, homesick for San Francisco after moving to Brooklyn Heights, wrote their famous paean to the "city by the bay . . . high on a hill . . . above the blue and windy sea." By 1962, when Tony Bennett's recording made the song world famous, the couple had moved back to the Bay Area, where Douglass died of a heart attack and George took his own life in grief a few years later.
Courtesy of SFHR, SFPL.

"A GAY BAR IN GAY SAN FRANCISCO . . . we follow Jamie to the Good Fairy Bar in San Francisco, along the docks of the Embarcadero and Fisherman's Wharf and then to Nob Hill . . . SAN FRANCISCO THE GAY CAPITAL. VISIT BARS. NOB HILL. WATERFRONT CRUISING. UNION SQUARE PARK. Let's take a visit to San Francisco and see why it's the gay boy's capital. ROUGH TRADE. PEEPING TOMS. CRUEL HUSTLERS."

—From *Bottoms Up,* 1966, by Ned Winslow.

lic about the "normalcy" of homosexuality and to provide lesbians and gay men with safe, discreet meeting places where they could socialize without the fear of police harassment that went hand in hand with bar patronage. The homophile movement also worked quietly within established social institutions to advance gay and lesbian causes, seeking out heterosexual allies in the medical, legal, religious, political, and scientific professions. While the homophile movement succeeded in securing limited civil rights and public acceptance of lesbians and gays who embraced mainstream cultural values, it did so at the expense of other queers who occupied more countercultural positions.

The earliest homophile group, the Mattachine Society, had been founded by Harry Hay and four other men in Los Angeles in 1950 and quickly established a number of chapters across the country, including in San Francisco and Berkeley. Sharp political differences between members in the early years of the organization resulted in the resignation of the Marxist-oriented founders and the relocation of

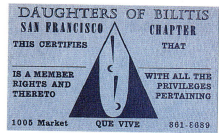

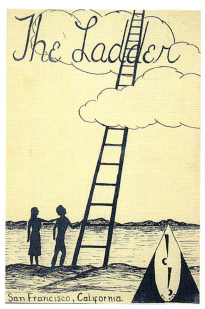

Top: *DOB membership card. The first national DOB convention, the first national lesbian conference, took place in San Francisco in May 1960.* Courtesy of GHLS.

Left and Above: The Ladder, *the monthly magazine of the DOB, began publication in October 1956.*

"'. . . Sponsored by the Glide Foundation of San Francisco and the Board of Christian Social Concerns of the Methodist Church, a four-day consultation May 30 through June 2 [1964] between members of the homophile community and representatives of various Protestant churches opened unexpected avenues of communication and an expression of continued cooperation between the two groups.' The resulting Council on Religion and the Homosexual was founded by Ted McIlvenna 'to promote a continuing dialogue between the religious community and the homosexual.'"

—Del Martin

"A Page in History," flyer, 1964.
Courtesy of GLHS.

A costume ball held on New Year's Day 1965 at California Hall to raise funds for the Council on Religion and the Homosexual, after attendees were harassed by police, became a turning point in the San Francisco gay rights movement. The ACLU took the case, which was dismissed. Photo credit: *San Francisco Examiner,* photo by Ray "Scotty" Morris.

the Mattachine Society's national offices to San Francisco by 1957. Under the direction of Hal Call, who had begun publishing the nationally distributed *Mattachine Review* in San Francisco in 1954, the homophile group's political ideology grew steadily more conservative—prefiguring in important ways the "Log Cabin" Republican stance adopted by a later generation of gays. Ironically, the Mattachine Society simultaneously came under surveillance by the federal government and was infiltrated by the FBI on the suspicion that it was a communist front organization. In 1955, San Franciscans Phyllis Lyon and Del Martin, along with three other lesbian couples, founded the Daughters of Bilitis (DOB), the first lesbian social and political organization in the United States. Besides chronicling many important political and social events in the 1950s and 1960s, the pages of the DOB journal *The Ladder* were filled with advice on how women who loved women could attain middle-class respectability if they gave up butch/femme styles associated with the more working-class lesbian bar culture.

An incident that forged lasting ties between the city's progressive political elements and the homophile movement took place on New Year's Day 1965. As a result of the black civil rights movement, a wave of social activism had spread through liberal members of the Protestant clergy during the early 1960s. In San Francisco, Glide Memorial Methodist Church, in the heart of the Tenderloin, was perfectly situated to become a center of progressive Christianity—especially since the Reverend Cecil Williams already had a history of activism there in the fight for racial equality. Ted McIlvenna, a young social worker at Glide, became sensitized to the potentially dire social and economic consequences of homosexuality when he began working with young gay hustlers—many who were escaping abusive homes. McIlvenna responded in December 1964 by organizing the Council on Religion and the Homosexual (CRH), which devoted itself to combating homophobia within the mainline churches and worked closely with the homophile groups. When the CRH held a benefit Mardi Gras Ball on January 1, 1965, the police showed up in force. Squad cars and paddy wagons lined the street in front of California Hall, even though all the proper permits had been secured by the organizers. Guests, many of them wearing drag in keeping with the spirit of the event, had to approach the building through a gauntlet of uniformed officers and were photographed as they arrived. Police arrested the CRH lawyers who tried to prevent them from entering the private event without a search warrant. Liberal heterosexual ministers

Background art: *Image from the Mattachine Society pamphlet describing San Francisco as the organization's national headquarters.*
Left: *Mattachine Logo*

"Under the benign attitude of the Christopher administration, those who practice sex deviation operate in San Francisco today to a shocking extent, under shocking circumstances, and in open and flagrant defiance of the law . . . So favorable is the official San Francisco climate for the activities of these persons that . . . an organization of sex deviates known as the Mattachine Society, whose national office is established in our city, *actually passed a resolution praising Mayor Christopher by name for what the resolution described as the enlightened attitude of his administration toward them.*"

—Russell L. Wolden,
The Truth About the Mayor's "Clean" City—
An Expose!
A radio speech on October 7, 1959.

41

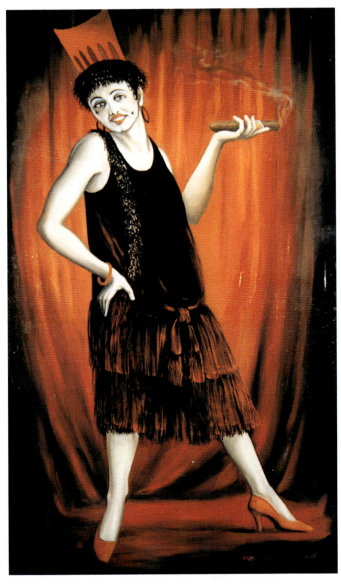

A portrait of José Sarria that hung in the Black Cat Cafe, where he performed his operatic comedies. Courtesy of GLHS.

witnessed firsthand the kind of official intimidation that constituted a regular feature of lesbian and gay social life, and, for the first time, voices that commanded a sense of social legitimacy began speaking out about anti-gay policies in San Francisco.

Lyon, Martin, Call, and their homophile associates made important inroads into San Francisco's political establishment—so much so that as early as 1959 mayoral candidate Russ Wolden had accused incumbent mayor George Christopher of allowing San Francisco to become "the national headquarters of organized homosexuals in the United States." Wolden's cynical campaign ploy backfired—Christopher had in fact orchestrated a draconian police crackdown on homosexual activity in the city during his administration—and had the unexpected consequence of galvanizing the lesbian and gay electorate. Surprisingly, the first gay venture into city politics came not from the homophile movement, but from the bar culture—and it came in the person of José Sarria, a flamboyant, charismatic, and immensely popular waiter and drag performer at the Black Cat. Cavorting about the cafe in various degrees of feminine apparel, Sarria had won a devoted following for the weekly satirical operatic revues he had staged since the early 1950s. His performances lampooned local anti-gay politics, but Sarria simultaneously chided gays who settled for second-class citizenship. He customarily ended his shows by requiring the audience to stand up, clasp hands, and join him in a rousing rendition of "God Save Us Nellie Queens" (sung to the tune of "My Country 'Tis of Thee"). Many then present remember finding in Sarria's performances the first inkling of what would later be called "gay pride." And when Sarria received 5,600 votes in his bid for the San Francisco Board of Supervisors in 1961, he provided the first solid evidence that gays and lesbians were a political constituency waiting to be tapped.

VOL. I NO. 1 DECEMBER 1964

BOOT PARTY   THURSDAYS

WHY NOT

518 ELLIS — PR 6-3333

Sarria's electoral campaign highlights perhaps the most distinctive quality of pre-Stonewall queer culture in the Bay Area. Elsewhere in the country, bar habitués and participants in the politically oriented homophile groups represented two distinct and sometimes mutually antagonistic subgroups. This was much less true in San Francisco, especially after Guy Strait formed the League for Civil Education (LCE) in 1961. The LCE sought to build up a gay voting block by recruiting and organizing in the bars, where its weekly *Citizen News,* the city's first gay tabloid, was distributed free of charge. An LCE spin-off group, the Society for Individual Rights (SIR), formed in 1964. SIR quickly became the largest homophile organization in the country, and its monthly magazine, *Vector,* was available on newsstands throughout the city. By 1967, the publication was carrying ads placed by mainstream politicians courting the gay and lesbian vote. That same year, SIR and the DOB began sponsoring well-attended Candidates Nights, where local office seekers could meet with their potential lesbian and gay constituencies.

In the early 1960s, gay community organizing revolved around the bars where much of gay life still transpired, and where homophobic oppression was most evident. The largest vice raid in San Francisco history took place in 1961, when police arrested 81 men and 14 women at the Tay-Bush Inn, an after-hours club that served beer and hamburgers to a mixed clientele. After first allowing "respectable looking" and politically well-connected customers to depart without incident, the police booked the largely queer, working-class, and dark-skinned remainder. Charges were dropped against all but two of the defendants, and the blatant prejudice manifested by the arrests helped shift public sympathies toward greater civil rights protection for homosexuals. Providing a backdrop for this and other similar vice busts was widespread official corruption that first came to light in the "gayola" scandal of 1961, in which SFPD and ABC officers were caught tak-

The Why Not? became San Francisco's first leather bar around 1961, followed soon thereafter by the Tool Box, which (in addition to the Jumping Frog on Polk Street, near Broadway) was featured in a 1964 Life magazine photo-essay that dubbed San Francisco the nation's "Gay Capital."

43

The California Motorcycle Club (which along with the Warlocks, was central to the gay biker, leather, and S/M subcultures) was founded circa 1960. Courtesy of Gayle Rubin.

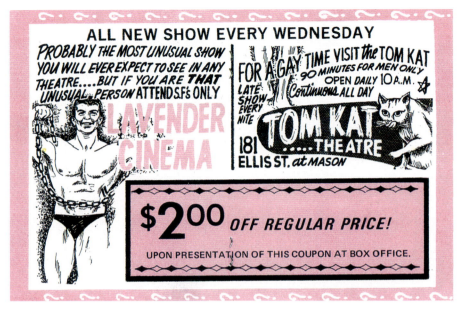

Although "hardcore" representations of sexual activity exist from the earliest days of the cinema, it was only in the late 1950s and early 1960s that feature-length narrative visual pornography began to play regularly in commercial movie houses. By the mid -'60s establishments like the Tom Kat Theatre could sustain themselves on exclusively gay porn films. From SFBay Underground Scene, pamphlet, courtesy of GLC, SFPL.

"Queer: A homosexual, or a practice that is generally associated with homosexuals. Not so scornful as in former years, it is still apt to cause a fight. Homosexuals often refer to each other by this term however. Has nothing to do with any role or any proclivity."

—*Dictionary of Gay Words and Phrases*
(San Francisco: Strait and Associates, 1964.)

ing bribes from gay bar owners in exchange for not raiding their bars. Acquittal of the principal figures in the scandal led bar owners in 1962 to form the Tavern Guild, the first gay business association in the United States. The Guild fought discriminatory practices by the liquor board and defended the right of their gay patrons to congregate. It retained a lawyer and bail bondsman to assist anyone arrested in the vicinity of a gay bar, and published a free brochure with legal information on what to do if arrested or harassed by the police. It bolstered its political clout by sponsoring popular community events like the annual Beaux Arts Ball and the Tavern Guild Picnic. Over the years, the Guild and the associated Imperial Court System developed into reliable mechanisms for charitable fund-raising and political leveraging within the queer community.

"Believing in our democratic heritage and that ethical values are self determined and limited only by every person's right to decide his own fate, we organize under this Constitution for: the reaffirming of individual pride and dignity regardless of orientation; the elimination of the public stigma attached to human self expression; the accomplishing of effective changes in unjust laws concerning private relationships among consenting adults; the giving of real and substantial aid to members in difficulties; the promoting of better physical, mental, and emotional health; the creating of a sense of community; and the establishing of an attractive social atmosphere and constructive outlets for members and friends.

—**Preamble of the Constitution of the Society for Individual Rights Charter,** dated July 20, 1964.

Right: *Tavern Guild Picnic, mid-1960s.* Courtesy of GLHS.

45

Pan-Graphics Press, operated by Hal Call of the Mattachine Society, was one of the earliest gay publishing ventures in San Francisco. In addition to offering hundreds of titles of interest to lesbian and gay readers through its mail-order catalogue, Pan-Graphics Press issued a number of volumes under its own imprimatur. Several of these were the published transcripts of "gay-friendly" radio or television shows produced in conjunction with homophile organizations. "The Homosexual in Our Society," for example, broadcast from KPFA in Berkeley on November 24, 1958, featured Blanche Baker, who wrote an advice column for a homophile newsletter, and Karl Bowman, former head of the Langley-Porter Clinic. "The Rejected" aired on KQED-TV in 1961 and featured such notables as anthropologist Margaret Mead and Evelyn Hooker, the psychiatrist who eventually persuaded her colleagues that homosexuality should not be considered a mental illness. Courtesy of GLHS.

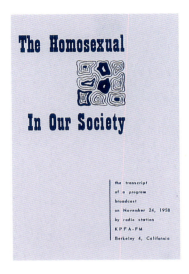

In the mid-'60s, *Life* magazine ran a multi-page pictorial about San Francisco that called it the "Gay Capital" of the United States—and the label rang true. Besides the bars, the city supported a growing number of movie theaters, bookstores, and small presses that catered to the queer population. Sympathetic local media coverage was becoming more routine. Lesbians and gays were more organized, more visible, and more vocal here than anywhere else in the country. They had hammered out a unique, mutually useful working relationship between homophile groups and bar-based constituencies. The two factions worked in concert to advance a civil rights agenda and expand the public space available to queer people. The Citizens' Alert, a 24-hour hotline that responded to incidents of police brutality against gays and lesbians, began operating in 1965. SIR opened the first gay community center in the nation on 6th Street in April 1966. The next month, on Armed Forces Day, a "Rally to Protest Exclusion of Homosexuals from the Armed Forces" was held on the steps of the Federal Building. Later that year, the

Gavin Arthur, grandson of U.S. President Chester A. Arthur, was a wealthy and eccentric San Francisco "bohemian" whose homosexuality was as well known as his penchant for Eastern religion. His pet theory was the "Circle of Sex," a means of classifying and arranging all the many varieties of human sexual identity.

August 22, 1966.

The National Planning Conference of Homophile Organizations, the first national convention of gay and lesbian groups, met in San Francisco. It later changed its name to North American Conference of Homophile Organizations (NACHO).

first national convention of lesbian and gay groups met in San Francisco, resulting in the formation of the North American Conference of Homophile Organizations (NACHO).

Just as San Francisco lesbians and gays were beginning to consolidate the gains they had made over the past two decades, the United States entered a period of dramatic social upheaval—racial tensions reached new heights, and an unpopular war in Vietnam began to escalate rapidly. The sense of vast, impending change hung almost palpably in the air. In an editorial in the *Citizen News* in August 1966, Guy Strait reflected upon the recent Watts uprising, the Free Speech Movement, and the many other instances of civil disobedience that were beginning to occur with greater frequency, before turning his thoughts toward the possibility of a more militant homosexual movement. "Sooner or later," he contended, "there is going to be a big push by homosexuals for rights and equality . . . When this big push comes along it is sure to bring police action against it. There will be some of the leaders of the homosexual movement that will be arrested. Some will be convicted. It is now that all of us must consider the possibility that one of our friends will be taken into custody for such action. Are we

1966.

Rikki Streicher opened Maud's Study, a popular lesbian bar, in the Haight in 1966.

Top Right: *Armed Forces Day Flyer.*
Courtesy of Gay/Lesbian Center, SFPL.

Right: *Lou Rand Hogan began writing about food and food preparation in 1947, and was eventually published in* Gourmet *and* Sunset *magazines.* The Gay Cookbook *(Sherbourne Press, 1965) "with campy cartoons by David Costain" went through four successful printings.* Courtesy of GLC, SFPL.

Far Right: *The Sirlebrity Capades was an annual fund-raising gala sponsored by the Society for Individual Rights. SIR was founded by young disaffected members of the older and more culturally conservative homophile groups, as the graphic design of this program cover suggests.* Courtesy of GLHS.

JUNE, 1966

★ RALLY ★
TO PROTEST EXCLUSION OF HOMOSEXUALS FROM THE ARMED SERVICES
MAY 21, 1966
(ARMED FORCES DAY)
2:00 P.M.

ON THE STEPS OF THE FEDERAL BUILDING 450 GOLDEN GATE AVENUE, SAN FRANCISCO

BE THERE FOR THIS HISTORIC EVENT!!!

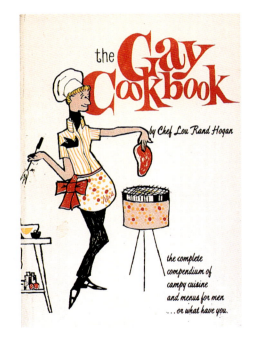

the Gay Cookbook

by Chef Lou Rand Hogan

the complete compendium of campy cuisine and menus for men ...or what have you.

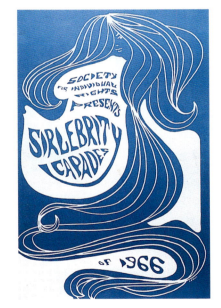

SOCIETY FOR INDIVIDUAL RIGHTS PRESENTS SIRLEBRITY CAPADES OF 1966

prepared to protect those who fight for our rights? Are we ready to realize that this person has sustained an injury in the field of battle?"

The same month that Strait's editorial ran in the *Citizen News,* an incident at Compton's Cafeteria at the corner of Turk and Taylor gave a sense of immediacy to his words. Compton's was frequented by Tenderloin street youth, queens, and hustlers whose age and poverty made it difficult to patronize the bars. One night, a police officer tried to grab one of the queens and, rather than put up with the harassment, she threw her coffee in the officer's face. Fighting erupted, and the management quickly closed the cafeteria. Angry young queer people broke out the windows, began throwing dishes and trays at the police, and burned down a nearby newsstand. The next day, Compton's refused to allow drag queens on the premises, and a picket line sprang up. That night, the cafeteria's newly installed plate glass windows were smashed once again. The days of gay militancy were much closer than Guy Strait envisioned. But it was not that the established leadership of the homophile movement suddenly turned radical, or that bar patrons got down off their stools and took to the streets. Rather, a new generation of queer people was beginning to make its presence felt.

"VANGUARD is an organization for the youth in the Tenderloin attempting to get its citizens a sense of dignity and responsibility too long denied.

"We of VANGUARD find our civil liberties imperiled by a hostile social order in which all difference from the usual in behavior is attacked. We find our rights as human beings scorned and ridiculed. We are forced to accept an unwarranted guilt which is more the product of society's hypocrisy than scientific fact" [1966].

Background art: *Vanguard Logo.*

Photo by Crawford Barton, Courtesy of GLHS.

Liberation and Assimilation, 1967–1981

"Gay liberation," a militant form of homosexual activism, emerged abruptly in the late 1960s. The older and more established homophile groups persevered with their methodical campaign to win social acceptance well into the 1970s—the Society for Individual Rights, for example, existed until 1978—but the more assertive, less apologetic style of the new liberation movement increasingly set the tone of queer activism. The attitudes of these two groups toward the American Psychiatric Association (APA) sharply delineate the differences in their respective methods. Homophiles had worked quietly behind the scenes since the 1950s to influence sympathetic members of the mental health profession to push for the depathologization of homosexuality. Then, on May 14, 1970, liberationists staged a "gay invasion" of the APA's annual meeting in San Francisco. The tactical and philosophical differences represented by these divergent approaches erupted into open conflict at the August 1970 convention of NACHO, the North American Conference of Homophile Organizations. Delegates split over such issues as whether to support the revolutionary Black Panther Party, or whether to allow straight people to participate in the gay movement.

December 15, 1973.

After nearly two decades of homophile pressure and three years of militant gay protest, homosexual orientation was removed from the American Psychiatric Association's *Diagnostic and Statistical Manual of Mental Disorders.*

Above: *The* Free Press, *a San Francisco gay newspaper, reports on "Friday of the Purple Hand."*
Courtesy of GLHS.

The disagreements were never successfully resolved, and NACHO disbanded shortly after the San Francisco convention.

The new style of activism represented a generational shift as much as a change of political sensibilities, signaling the coming-of-age of post–World War II baby boomers. Gay liberation certainly built upon the foundations laid by earlier generations, but it also drew inspiration from the youth counterculture and the many radical movements of the late 1960s and early 1970s. This was especially true in the Bay Area, where the sheer density of urban social space compelled various subcultures to overlap, intersect, and cross-fertilize one another. Psychedelic aesthetics, student unrest, the tactics of the civil rights struggle and black militancy, labor organizing, social critiques rooted in the anti-war movement, the second wave of feminism, and Marxist political analysis all contributed to the rise of the gay liberation movement. In turn, a new generation of gay activists added their energy and voices to other struggles with which they felt common cause.

The Committee for Homosexual Freedom (CHF), organized in the spring of 1969, was the first gay liberation group in the Bay Area. The CHF's most productive action was the picket it organized at States Steamship Lines to protest the firing of Gale Whitington, an employee who came out about his sexuality in a Berkeley newspaper. For weeks, gays picketed the company's offices every workday between noon and one. In the process, they began to grasp what it might be like to live openly homosexual lives and to sense the tremendous potential for social change their new movement had begun to tap. The CHF subsequently organized demonstrations at Tower Records, Safeway stores, Macy's, and the Federal Building to protest other instances of discrimination. By the summer of 1969, of course, gay protests were not unique to the Bay Area—the police raid at the Stonewall Inn on Christopher Street in New York City had helped crystalize a nationwide gay liberation movement. Ironically, many of the issues that fueled the Stonewall Uprising, such as indiscriminate police raids and harassment of gay bar patrons, had been countered successfully in San Francisco many years before due to effective organizing by groups like the Tavern Guild. Nevertheless, new militant groups sprang up around the Bay Area virtually overnight, with names like "Students for Gay Power," "Gay Women's Liberation," "Lavender Panthers," the "Gay Activists Alliance," and the ubiquitous "Gay Liberation Front."

"San Francisco is a refugee camp for homosexuals."

—Carl Wittman, *A Gay Manifesto*, 1970

"I guess homosexual freedom is the next battle for the Revolution. I'll help in every way I can."

—San Francisco Attorney Terrence Hallinan, CHF Newsletter, May 13, 1969.

"The Repression of homosexuals is a crime which cries to Heaven for vengeance. It is unnatural. It is a tyranny which directs itself to the destruction of human personality, a conspiracy of fear and ignorance that we can no longer bear, a scandal in a society which professes freedom as its most cherished ideal, and a fatal disease in the academic community, which professes to exist only to search for knowledge and truth. To wage war against that oppression, and the attitudes and fear behind it, we form the SGP."

—Statement of Purpose of the Students for Gay Power, in papers filed on October 24, 1969, seeking recognition as an officially recognized student organization at UC Berkeley.

3,000 "liberated" gays were among the 175,000 people who attended the massive peace rally in Golden Gate Park on March 24, 1971.

For all its radical rhetoric, gay liberation in the Bay Area relied primarily on picketing, publishing, and public assembly to advance its causes. The first act of violence associated with the organized movement was perpetrated by anti-gay bigots in October 1969. During a peaceful demonstration at the *San Francisco Examiner* offices to protest an article containing offensive stereotypes of gay men, lesbians, and transgendered people, an *Examiner* employee leaned out of a second-story window and heaved a bag of printer's ink onto the protesters below. As angry demonstrators began using the ink to write "Fuck the Examiner" and "Gay is Good" on the building's walls, police moved in to make arrests and a riot ensued. One demonstrator had his teeth kicked out by rampaging officers, while another was charged with obstructing traffic for falling down in the street while police beat her. The attack on the demonstrators sparked another protest the next day at City Hall, where a handful of activists shouting "Power to the People" staged a successful sit-in at the mayor's office before being taken into custody.

The gay liberation movement sought to align itself with other progressive social movements that fought dominance based on race and gender, but it all too often reproduced the very oppression it ostensibly sought to overturn. Although many people of color participated in gay liberation, the movement remained predominantly white. Queers of color often did not have the opportunity to address issues of sexuality in isolation from their other concerns and, unlike many whites,

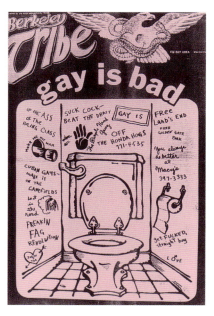

"We should try to form a working coalition with the Gay liberation and Women's liberation groups. We must always handle social forces in the most appropriate manner. And this is really a significant part of the population, both women and the growing number of homosexuals, that we have to deal with . . . ALL POWER TO THE PEOPLE!"

—Huey P. Newton,
Supreme Commander of the Black Panther Party, "A Letter from Huey to the Revolutionary Brothers and Sisters about the Women's Liberation and Gay Liberation Movements," *The Black Panther*, August 21, 1970, p. 5.

could not make being gay the principal focus of their struggles. Moreover, gay and lesbian culture could be every bit as racist as the dominant society. Just because white queers were learning to resist one form of oppression that personally affected them did not guarantee they understood their role in perpetuating other forms of oppression.

The rise of a separatist lesbian feminist movement reflected similar issues. Within the homophile movement, women and men had tended to work in parallel, and the most radical thrust of gay liberation had always addressed women's issues. But with the emergence of a powerful feminist movement in 1969 and 1970, some lesbians began to forge alliances with other women's groups. This was partly a response to the masculinist biases of the sexual revolution. Many radical males simply failed to comprehend that the open expression of sexuality might have different implications for women than it did for men. While it would not be accurate to characterize all feminism as implicitly supportive of lesbianism (or les-

Above Left: *Events in the Bay Area were quickly incorporated into national consciousness. The "Gay is Angry" calendar, published in New York, included many Bay Area events that were perceived to have national significance.*

Above Right: *In the streetwise vernacular of the time, "Gay is Bad" was just another way of saying "Gay is Good." The various graffiti refer to events of the day.* Courtesy of GLHS.

"The daily noontime picketing at States Steamship Company, 320 California Street, has become a groovin' spiritual happening. The morale of the picketers has much improved as has the great springtime weather. The size of the line remains undiminished as dedicated CHF members carry on the only really homosexual activist campaign in quite awhile. Every day, picketers sing freedom songs, and songs of joy and love, while they enjoy the sun, hold hands, and do what comes naturally. In fact, the picketers on California Street are acting in public just as all homosexuals have been saying for years that we should be able to act in public. They are acting out that statement: People are ready for their freedom when they assume it."

—*CHF Newsletter*, May 20, 1969.

The Gay Asian Information Network founded in Sunnyvale in 1977, the Gay Asian Association active at UC Berkeley in the late 1970s, and the Asian-American Alliance that existed in San Francisco in 1979–80 were the first known groups that addressed the needs of queer Asian Americans.

Far Left: *Guy Strait had published periodicals of interest to the homosexual community in the 1960s and 1970s, including the* LCE News, Town Talk, Cruise News, *and the* Bar Rag. *The* Maverick, *in addition to covering the Haight-Ashbury scene, ran such tongue-in-cheek features as whether drag was a communist conspiracy, or whether Ronald Reagan was a lesbian.* Courtesy of GLHS.

Left: *Asian American man protesting racial discrimination in Castro bars after having been asked for multiple pieces of identification and refused admission.* Courtesy of GLHS.

Opposite Page: *"Homosexual Freedom—Gay Strike—Picket Mon. Thru Friday—Picket 12 till 1—320 California Street—Committee For Homosexual Freedom—Come With Us."*

bianism as implicitly feminist), it would be fair to say that shared experiences of oppression based on gender enabled lesbian feminists to find more in common with other politicized women than most gay men did with other males. Lesbians made important contributions to the distinctive women's culture that blossomed in the early 1970s, a culture with its own music, literature, social theories, gathering places, community publications, fairs, and festivals. Olivia Records, the women's recording label based in Oakland, characterized the women's movement in its heyday. The Women's Building in the Mission District was first conceived in the 1970s and continues to embody the ethos of the women's movement today. Separatist culture provided many women with an opportunity to gain economic independence by learning to work in trades from which they had traditionally been excluded; it helped them organize for their own physical self-defense, and it gave

Gay American Indians, the first gay American Indian liberation organization, was founded in San Francisco by Randy Burns (Top) *and Barbara Cameron,* (Above) *in July 1975.* Photograph by Rink Foto.

Above Right: *The Gay Latino Alliance (GALA) was organized in 1975.* Photograph © by Cathy Cade.

many their first glimpse of what childbirth and child rearing might look like outside the context of the patriarchal nuclear family.

The consolidation of a feminist alliance between lesbians and straight women depended on a gender ideology that regarded gender itself as inherently oppressive. The task of women's liberation was thus to overthrow the gender system and to open up for both women and men new possibilities for attaining a more fully human form of personhood. One of the repercussions of this new vision was the marginalization of traditional butch/femme roles in the lesbian community and the disparagement of drag among gay men. Transsexuals suffered, too, often being ostracized by women's groups due to the belief that transsexuals perpetrated the very gender stereotypes that needed to be overthrown. Being driven to the periphery of lesbian and gay culture accelerated the formation of a distinctive transgender community in the years that followed. Not all elements of the queer community embraced the new gender ideology, however, or adhered to a standard of political correctness that mandated one proper response to gender-based oppres-

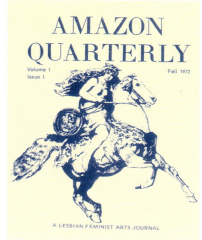

Above: Amazon Quarterly, *one of many lesbian separatist publications produced in the Bay Area in the 1970s.* Courtesy of GLC, SFPL.

Left: *Some participants in the Women's Movement empowered themselves by learning traditionally male trades.* Photograph © by Cathy Cade.

sion. Radical "genderfuck" groups like the Cockettes, the Angels of Light, and the Sisters of Perpetual Indulgence offered another, more playful, approach to resisting the coerciveness of the gender system.

S/M practices met a fate similar to transgenderism in the 1970s. In spite of leather's outlaw image, an S/M lifestyle was never as marginalized in the gay men's community as it was among women. Women who practiced S/M were doubly liable for censure by "vanilla" lesbians—not only for eroticizing politically suspect role-playing activities, but for having internalized patriarchal notions about violence and domination. Sadomasochists, like transgenderists, responded by beginning to build networks along lines other than sexual orientation. When the Society

January 11, 1970.

The *Gay Bay* newsletter published
an article in which it claims that
in response to a widely publicized
demonstration sponsored by Gay
Women's Liberation to protest discrimination against women in a UC
Berkeley karate class in January
1970, KGO-TV aired an editorial
stating that any woman who would
publicly open her mouth in protest
had lost her femininity. The editorial
also stated that it was better for
women not to learn karate, so that
they would be more susceptible to
rape, which would encourage them
to become mothers and stay at home.
Members of other feminist groups
joined Gay Women's Liberation in a
subsequent demonstration at KGO-TV
studios.

"The first Lesbian Political Exploration happened Oct. 25, 1975 and brought together over 250 women. The day-long conference centered around general questions in an effort to lay groundwork for future united action based on our common struggle, and to open up the lines of communication among actively political Lesbians who are working all over the Bay Area and are dedicated to changing the system."

—Nancy Adair [and others],
The First Lesbian Political Exploration,
a pamphlet, 1975.

Opposite Page Top: *A women's self-defense class.*

Opposite Page Bottom: *A women's music festival near Santa Cruz, circa 1974.*

Photographs © by Cathy Cade.

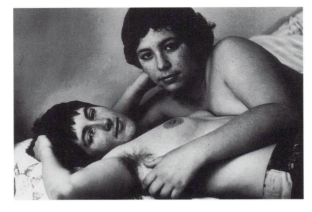

Background art: *From the* Effeminist, *a newsletter for "gay men interested in the feminist revolution," was priced at "10¢ to women, children, old men, Third World, and gay men" and "25¢ to known straight white males."*

Bay Area–based Golden Gate Girls was a support group and social organization for male cross-dressers and male-to-female transsexuals. Responding to inquiries from female-to-male (FTM) individuals, the group expanded its name to Golden Gate Girls/Golden Gate Guys and became one of the earliest transgender organizations in the United States to address FTM needs.
Photographs by Crawford Burton.

of Janus was founded in San Francisco in 1974 as a "pansexual" organization for sadomasochists of all genders and orientations, it was the first such organization on the West Coast, and only the second in the world. Members of Cardea, Janus's women's focus group, formed the nucleus of the leatherdyke community that has become such a distinctive feature of Bay Area S/M culture.

While narrowly focused campaigns like the States Line picket continued to play an important role in San Francisco's liberation movement, Bay Area gay liberationists increasingly found themselves backed up by the courts and the political process. Gays who had protested bathroom harassment at Macy's since the 1960s won an important case in 1973 when the California Supreme Court ruled in their favor, making it illegal for police to spy on public-restroom behavior. Another ongoing campaign against Pacific Telephone met with similar success due to increased lesbian and gay involvement in local government. The phone company had refused to list SIR in the yellow pages because their ad contained the word "homophile"; SIR protested, but the Public Utilities Commission upheld the phone company's position. A series of large demonstrations outside phone company offices in 1973 protesting the yellow pages issue as well as an explicitly anti-gay hiring policy produced no results. The San Francisco Human Rights Commission (HRC) finally intervened. The Board of Supervisors had established a gay advisory board to the HRC in 1975, and the

Anton Dunnigan (Reggie) of the Cockettes and Adrian Brooke of the Angels of Light, backstage at the Angels of Light's Mindkamp Kabaret in August 1976. Along with the Sisters of Perpetual Indulgence, the Cockettes and the Angels of Light, defined the meaning of "genderfuck." Photograph by Daniel Nicoletta.

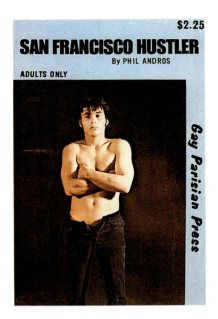

$2.25

SAN FRANCISCO HUSTLER
By PHIL ANDROS

ADULTS ONLY

Gay Parisian Press

San Francisco Hustler *(Parisian Press, 1971), by the male hustler Phil Andros, one of nearly 25 pseudonyms used by Samuel Steward. After establishing himself as the tattoo artist Phil Sparrow and moving to Oakland, Steward befriended many hustlers. In addition to erotica, he also published novels, short stories, poetry, and such nonfiction as* Dear Sammy: Letters from Gertrude Stein and Alice B. Toklas, *chronicling his friendship with the former Bay Area residents.* Courtesy of GLC, SFPL.

Opposite page: *San Francisco's first openly gay elected official, Supervisor Harvey Milk, marches with supporters from Castro to City Hall, January 9, 1978.* Photograph by Rink Foto.

seasoned activists who constituted the board helped persuade city government to take a stand. In May 1975, the Board of Supervisors ordered Pacific Telephone to comply with a municipal ordinance prohibiting employment discrimination based on sexual orientation. When the phone company refused, the Board of Supervisors threatened to revoke city contracts. In October, after being given 30 days to either comply or begin removing its public telephones from San Francisco, Pacific Telephone finally capitulated.

The election of liberal Mayor George Moscone in 1975 represented a significant shift in queer access to city government in San Francisco. In the first few months of the Moscone administration, a number of gay and lesbian leaders moved into appointed positions. Electoral successes soon followed. Harvey Milk, the owner of a camera store on Castro Street, had been marching steadily toward office for years. In 1973, Milk finished tenth in the field with approximately 17,000 votes. He finished seventh in a race for six seats in 1975, receiving 52,649 votes. After an unsuccessful bid for the state assembly, Milk eventually won a seat on the San Francisco Board of Supervisors in 1977 to become the first openly gay elected official in the city's history. On the day of his inauguration—January 9, 1978— Milk led a procession of tens of thousands of his supporters from Castro Street to City Hall.

These political accomplishments would not have been possible without the organized, geographically concentrated constituency that began to take shape in the early 1970s. At the beginning of the decade, Polk Street, Haight-Ashbury, the Tenderloin, and South of Market were the principal gay and lesbian enclaves, while the Castro was still a predominantly straight neighborhood. Four gay bars (in addition to three others in the vicinity) opened in the Castro in the summer of 1971, signaling the area's shifting demographics. The advent of the Castro Street Fair in 1974 added to the queer ambiance. So did the refurbishing of the run-down Castro Theater—which quickly earned its reputation as San Francisco's premier repertory theater by catering to audiences attuned to the coded, campy nuances of classic Hollywood films. By 1977, a thriving gay economy in the Castro generated $25 to $30 million annually. San Francisco's queer population grew explosively throughout the 1970s, as the city's reputation for toleration drew lesbians and gay men from around the world. The Department of Public Health estimated the queer population of San Francisco at 90,000 in 1972; by 1977, the *Chronicle* put the fig-

1970.
Sally Gearhart and Rick Stokes became the first open homosexuals hired by the city of San Francisco when they served in the Family Services Administration in 1970.

February 8, 1972.
The Alice B. Toklas Democratic Club, the first gay Democratic club in California, was formed from SIR's political committee by Jim Foster. As one of two San Francisco delegates to the Democratic National Convention in Miami, Foster delivered a nationally televised speech on behalf of gay rights in July 1972.

ure at 120,000. A year later, it revised its estimate upward to 150,000 people with a combined annual purchasing power of $1.4 billion. Political influence developed apace with economic and demographic growth. In 1974, 40,000 lesbian and gay voters turned out for the fall elections, representing 12 percent of all votes cast. Politicians simply could not afford to ignore queer interests in San Francisco.

The annual Freedom Day celebration, held during the third weekend in June each year to commemorate the Stonewall Uprising, is the most visible tip of the Bay Area's queer culture. On June 27, 1970, 20 to 30 people marched down

"... We do not knowingly hire or retain in our employment persons—and this could include homosexuals—whose reputation, performance, or behavior would impose a risk to our customers, other employees, or to the reputation of the company ..."

—The Pacific Telephone and
Telegraph Company,
October 8, 1970.

September 8, 1975.

Leonard Matlovich was featured on the cover of *Time* magazine with the headline "I Am a Homosexual: The Gay Drive for Acceptance." The gay Air Force sergeant was in the midst of a legal battle to be reinstated in the armed forces. The article thrust him into the limelight and he became a gay media hero, the subject of an NBC made-for-TV movie, and eventually ran (unsuccessfully) for political office in San Francisco.

Right: *The first annual Castro Street Fair, spearheaded by Harvey Milk, was held in August 1974.*

Opposite Page Left: *Image from the Castro in mid-'70s.*
Photographs by Crawford Barton. Courtesy of GLHS.

Gay-In Poster
Courtesy of GLHS.

Polk Street from Aquatic Park to City Hall in San Francisco's first gay rights march, but it was a small affair compared to the "Gay-In" held at Golden Gate Park the next day. There was no organized public commemoration of Stonewall in San Francisco the next year. Instead, Bay Area gays and lesbians joined a statewide rally in Sacramento to support Willie Brown's consenting-adults bill, which would decriminalize private sexual acts performed between consenting partners. In 1972, however, 50,000 people turned out for "Christopher Street West." In 1973, the "Gay Freedom Day Parade," as the event was officially known that year, competed with a rival "Festival of Gay Liberation" held at the Civic Center. A few months later, the Pride Foundation, a new nonprofit multiservice organization, was formed partly to coordinate future events and avoid similar conflicts. By 1975, the gay parade had become the largest such event in the nation, and the largest parade in San Francisco. It drew 80,000 attendees that year (more than the Chinese New Year Parade), and 200,000 in 1977—twice as large as the first National March on Washington for Lesbian and Gay Rights in 1979.

Images from the Castro in mid-'70s. Photographs by Crawford
Barton. Courtesy of GLHS.

CHRISTOPHER STREET-WEST/SF

"The last Sunday in June is fast becoming The Gay Freedom Day. Commemorations of the Christopher Street Stonewall Riot have been seen in many places, and more and more areas are planning observances. However anyone may feel about Gay Liberation, all homosexuals have benefited by its coming.

"Nevertheless, liberation is not a static thing! It is neither complete nor over, but ongoing, and it is different things to different people. The process of raising the level of consciousness of both Gay and Straight continues. The parade in San Francisco can be a major vehicle for this purpose. In an election year it is desirable to manifest an image of strength and solidarity.

"OPPRESSION comes from without! That is not to say that gays do not oppress other gays, they do, but it is the larger society that visits OPPRESSION upon all of us. There are many forms of OPPRESSION, but the core of it all is a hate-filled lack of consideration for the individuality of others, for their feelings, their wishes, their persons, their property, their very being. We invite all who care about their Gay Brothers and Sisters to join with us in celebrating Christopher Street Liberation Day, June 25, 1972. If the parade is not to your liking, for any of a variety of reasons, then come to our meetings and discuss the difficulties, present alternatives.

"This is a celebration for the Community. It is a joyous outpouring of our gayness for all the world to see, in whatever form we feel that gayness takes. It belongs to all Gays, though the radical militants would seem to have slightly more claim, by right of origin, since it is their physical actions we commemorate. Yet, they were only the agents of all Gays, living and dead, and yet unborn, in whose name they smashed OPPRESSION in the snout. The curses have been shouted, the rocks have been thrown, the fires have been lit and put out, but the Gay Pride born on Christopher Street in June of 1969 goes on. This is what we celebrate, this is why we parade: this belongs to all of us, and all who come to celebrate our Gay Liberation with us are welcome, indeed!"

Gay Sunshine *debuted in August, 1970, when the new (straight) owners of the White Horse tried to ban distribution of the newspaper in the Bay Area's oldest gay bar. Patrons protested. Pictured above is volume 1, number 2, which shows the victory celebration when the owners relented.* Gay Sunshine *publisher Winston Leyland went on to found Gay Sunshine Press, the oldest surviving gay book publisher in the country.*

San Francisco's Gay Freedom Day Parade on June 25, 1978, drew an estimated 350,000 marchers, incensed by the spate of recent gay rights defeats across the country and by the new threat from California's Proposition 6. For the parade, Gilbert Baker designed the first rainbow flag, which became an international symbol of lesbian and gay pride. Initially designed with eight stripes (hot pink=sex, red=life, orange=healing, yellow=sun, green=serenity with nature, turquoise=art, indigo=harmony, violet=spirit), it was reduced to six stripes in 1982 for ease of manufacturing. 1978 also marked Jon Reed Sims's founding of the San Francisco Gay Freedom Day Marching Band & Twirling Corps, the first lesbian and gay musical organization in the world.

The parade culminated in a rally at City Hall, where Harvey Milk told the marchers: "I want to recruit you. I want to recruit you for the fight to preserve your democracy from the John Briggs and the Anita Bryants who are trying to constitutionalize bigotry. We are not going to allow that to happen. We are not going to sit back in silence as 300,000 of our gay brothers and sisters did in Nazi Germany. We are not going to allow our rights to be taken away and then marched with bowed heads into the gas chambers. On this anniversary of Stonewall, I ask my gay sisters and brothers to make the commitment to fight. For themselves. For their freedom. For their country."

Along with the parade, other landmark institutions of the Bay Area's contemporary queer culture took root in the 1970s. The influential *Gay Sunshine* began publishing in 1970. Though the newspaper folded after two decades, many of its contemporary publications remain viable today. The *Bay Area Reporter* (B.A.R.), whose acronym points to the paper's historic ties to the city's bar culture, began publishing in 1971. *The San Francisco Sentinel* debuted in 1974, and the *Bay Times* (originally called *Coming Up!*) first appeared on newsstands in 1979. Queer arts flourished just as the queer press did. *Tales of the City,* Armistead Maupin's fictionalized account of the lesbian and gay milieu he and his extensive readership called home, first appeared in the *Chronicle* in 1976. The world's first gay film festival, which later evolved into Frameline's annual San Francisco International Lesbian and Gay Film Festival, took place in 1977. Theatre Rhinoceros was also founded in 1977. Beyond the arts, other fixtures of the community established themselves. The Metropolitan Community Church, a spiritual home for many who felt alienated from their religious heritages due to sexual orientation, was founded in 1970. The Community Softball League started up in 1973. Bars and bathhouses—the mainstay institutions of earlier lesbian and gay cultural life—continued to thrive in the early years of the liberation movement, and many other types of businesses sprang up to create even more varied kinds of semipublic queer social space. More than 560 bars, baths, dance clubs, coffee houses, bookstores, theaters, and gyms catering to lesbian and gay clientele came and went during the 1970s.

Above: *On February 9, 1977, the Gay Film Festival of Super-8 Films was held at the Bay Area Gay Liberation Community Center at 32 Page Street. The free screening of experimental films was so overwhelmingly popular that the program was repeated the following month at the larger Pride Foundation Community Center at 330 Grove Street. The event marked the beginning of the San Francisco International Lesbian and Gay Film Festival, the oldest continuing lesbian and gay film festival in the world.* Courtesy of GLHS.

Left: *Gay Freedom Celebration 1973*

71

Above: *The* Bay Area Reporter *(B.A.R.),
begun in April 1971 by Bob Ross, is the
longest continuously published gay newspaper
in San Francisco and one of the oldest gay
newspapers in the country.*

Right: *The first installment of Armistead
Maupin's serial novel* Tales of the City
*appeared in the May 25, 1976, San
Francisco Chronicle. When published as a
book in 1978, it became a national best-seller.*
Courtesy of GLC, SFPL.

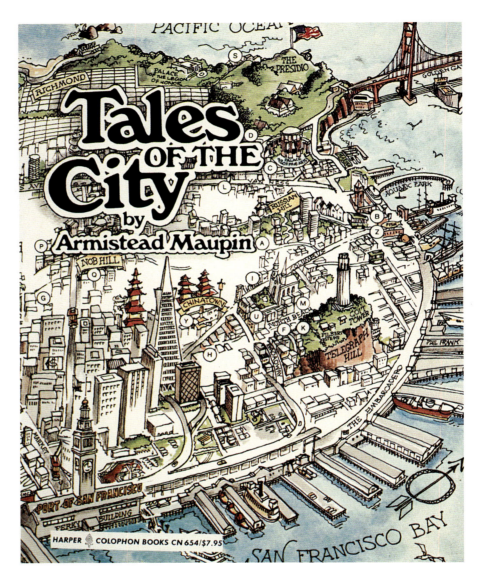

Left: *After premiering at the Castro Theatre on December 1, 1977,* Word Is Out, *the pioneering documentary by Peter Adair and the Mariposa Group, was distributed nationally. Members included (from left) Lucy Massie Phenix, Nancy Adair, Peter Adair, Rob Epstein, Andrew Brown, and Veronica Selver.*

1972.

Achvah Chutzpah, the first Gay Jewish organization in the United States, was founded in San Francisco in 1972. Sha'ar Zahav, the predominantly queer congregation that publishes the monthly *Jewish Gaily Forward,* started in 1977. A third congregation, Ahvat Shalom, was organized in 1982.

1979.

CUAV (Commmunity United Against Violence) was founded in 1979. Lester Olmstead-Rose has been its guiding force for many years.

The cultural visibility, political clout, economic strength, and civil rights victories that grew out of gay liberation were not achieved without cost. While queer people have long been the targets of hate crimes and other forms of discrimination, anti-queer violence escalated in reaction to the increased presence of lesbians and gays in public life. Police sweeps remained commonplace in areas where sexuality could come under surveillance. A Tenderloin sweep on November 11, 1971, for example, netted 46 transgender sex workers, while another sweep in March the next year resulted in the arrest of over 300 men and women. In response to ongoing police harassment, gay activists agitated for better communication between the SFPD and members of the community. Before the decade was over, not only did the police department require its officers to attend sexual orientation sensitivity training, it actively recruited gay cops. Still, anti-gay crime remained high

1972.

San Francisco City College offered Gay Literature, the first course of its kind, before Jack Collins went on to establish the Department of Gay and Lesbian Studies, the first in the United States.

September 1974.

The premier issue of *Journal of Homosexuality* was published, edited by John De Cecco, who also established a center for the study of sexuality at San Francisco State University.

1974.

The Golden Gate Business Association, an important gay and lesbian business organization, was formed.

July 1977.

Bay Area Physicians for Human Rights was formed by gay doctors wanting to improve medical care for gay people.

Above: Crimes Against Nature *was one of the most powerful works of gay theater to appear in the 1970s.* Courtesy of GLHS

GAY MEN'S THEATER COLLECTIVE
CRIMES AGAINST NATURE

Gumption Theater
1563 Page (nr. Masonic)
San Francisco

Thursday—Sunday
October 13—December 11
8:30 PM

$3.00 Donation
Information: 421-7333 x 9
Free childcare Saturday nights

Benefit Performance
Jeanne Jullion Defense Fund
Thanksgiving Night, Nov. 24

a play by faggots about survival

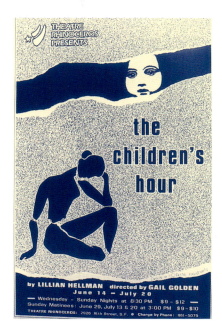

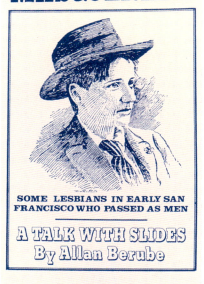

Far Left Top: *Liberty Baths*

Far Left Bottom: *Alan Estes and Lanny Banquiet founded Theatre Rhinoceros, one of the best known and most successful gay theater companies, on January 1, 1977.* Poster design by Corinne Haverinen. Courtesy of GLHS.

Left: *Lesbian Masquerade, a lecture and slide show by Allan Bérubé, represented the collective labor of the San Francisco Lesbian and Gay History Project, one of the earliest grassroots efforts in the nation to undertake the serious scholarly investigation of the queer past. Many members of the group later pioneered university-based lesbian and gay studies programs.* Courtesy of GLHS.

June 21, 1977.

Four youths screaming "Faggot, faggot, faggot!" and "This one's for Anita!" murdered gardener Robert Hillsborough in the Mission District. Mayor Moscone ordered flags flown at half-mast the day of the funeral, which attracted 3,000 mourners to Grace Cathedral.

Proposition 6, an initiative sponsored by State Senator John Briggs to expel gay and lesbian teachers from the school system as well as to forbid homosexuality from being presented in a positive light, was defeated on November 7, 1978, after an arduous media campaign. Photograph courtesy of GLHS.

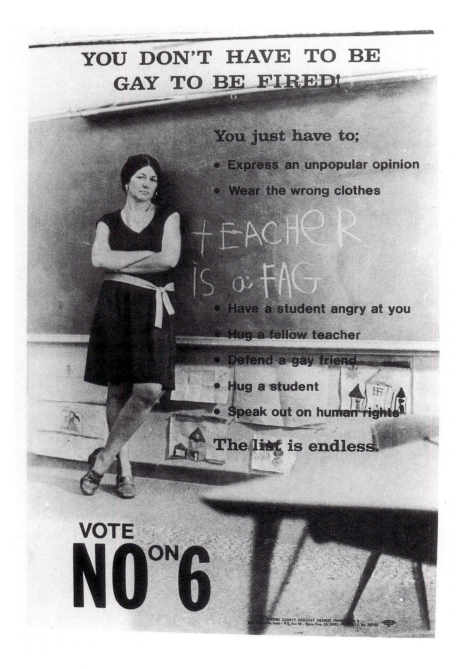

76

"IF THEY COME FOR ME IN THE NIGHT" "THEY'LL COME FOR YOU IN THE MORNING."

©1978 TOO MUCH GRAPHICS   PHOTO: MARC HUESTIS/"UNITY"

FIGHT BRIGGS / NO ON 6 AND 7

Left: *A poster from the media campaign to fight the Briggs Initiative.* Courtesy of GLHS.

Below: *Statewide Workers Conference Against Briggs.* Courtesy of GLHS.

and police protection could never be assumed. Indeed, the police were often the antagonists. The Reverend Ray Broshears, one of the most active gay liberationists of the early 1970s, used his weekly radio show on KSAN to publicize a memorial service for gays slain by the police in Berkeley and Los Angeles—and promptly lost his broadcast slot. In 1979, drunken off-duty police officers participated in vandalizing Peg's Place, a lesbian bar on Geary Street.

Gay murders occurred with frightening regularity—by 1976, they accounted for 10 percent of the city's homicide rate, compelling the SFPD to set up a special investigative squad. Between 1973 and 1976, a mass murderer known as "The Doodler" (for his characteristic knife mutilations of the victims) stalked San Francisco's gay bars. The suspected perpetrator, identified by the few men who survived his attacks, could not be prosecuted because evidence against him was obtained illegally. Gay businesses were frequent targets of bombings and arson. One gay bar, Toad Hall, was burned out three times in three months during 1973. The Metropolitan Community Church was set ablaze in 1972 and 1973, resulting in over $100,000 of damage each time. Arson fires at the Ritch Street Baths, Castro Rock Steam Baths, and the Turkish Baths in 1977 and 1978 each left one

STATEWIDE WORKERS CONFERENCE AGAINST BRIGGS / PROP 6

SAT & SUN, SEPT 9 & 10, 1978
MISSION HIGH, 18th & DOLORES, SAN FRANCISCO
South of Market Cultural Center, Brannan between 8th & 9th
DANCE SATURDAY NIGHT
INFO & CHILDCARE: 552-5245, 285-1803
DONATIONS AT THE DOOR

dead. Just after the Pride Day festivities in 1977, firebombs exploded in five gay-owned businesses South of Market. Someone set off canisters of tear gas at the annual Halloween celebration on Polk Street that year, and the number of muggings increased dramatically.

The increasing frequency of isolated acts of intimidation and hatred coincided with the emergence of a nationwide anti-gay backlash. Former Miss America Anita Bryant led a 1977 campaign to repeal a gay rights ordinance already on the books in Dade County, Florida. Distorted images of San Francisco, depicted as a "cesspool of sexual perversion gone rampant," figured prominently in the Dade County contest. Bay Area residents responded by raising funds to help fight the conservative forces in Florida, but the ordinance was overturned by a two to one margin—the first time hard-won protective legislation for lesbians and gays had been rolled back. A boycott of Florida orange juice did, however, result in Bryant's ouster as the spokesperson for the Florida Citrus Growers Association. Heartened by the conservative victory in the South, reactionary forces in California wasted no time in launching an anti-gay offensive of their own. Just two days after the Dade County vote, California State Senator John Briggs announced Proposition 6, a statewide initiative that would forbid lesbians and gay men from teaching in California public schools. Queers wasted no time in organizing effective opposition, resulting in the defeat of the measure by a 58 percent No vote a year later. The campaign against the Briggs Initiative was an important victory for lesbians and gay men, coming at a time when, after a decade of divisive cultural and political upheaval, the national mood was becoming increasingly intolerant and illiberal.

The anti-gay backlash reached its nadir three weeks after the Briggs Initiative went down to defeat. On November 21, 1978, former SFPD officer and San Francisco City Supervisor Dan White gunned down Supervisor Harvey Milk and Mayor George Moscone in Moscone's offices in San Francisco City Hall. Retracing the path they had taken a scant 11 months earlier when Milk had taken office, tens of thousands of mourners marched from the Castro to the Civic Center for a spontaneous candlelight vigil at which Joan Baez sang. Grief turned to outrage on May 21, 1979, when White was convicted of manslaughter rather than first-degree murder and received a surprisingly lenient sentence. The jury accepted the improbable "twinkie defense," concluding that White was not fully respon-

Photograph by Rink Foto.

MAYOR, MILK SLAIN; DAN WHITE SEIZED

San Francisco Examiner **EXTRA**

114th Year No. 145   Monday, November 27, 1978   20¢   R

I Was
There
May 21
WHITE NIGHT
1979

SFPD

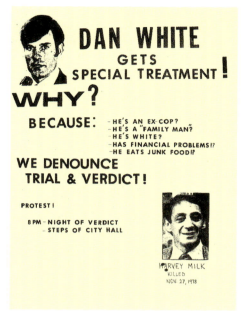

DAN WHITE
GETS
SPECIAL TREATMENT!

WHY?

BECAUSE: - HE'S AN EX-COP?
- HE'S A "FAMILY MAN?"
- HE'S WHITE?
- HAS FINANCIAL PROBLEMS!?
- HE EATS JUNK FOOD!?

WE DENOUNCE
TRIAL & VERDICT!

PROTEST!

8 PM - NIGHT OF VERDICT
- STEPS OF CITY HALL

HARVEY MILK
KILLED
NOV. 27, 1978

Far Left: *Burning police cars from a distance.* Photograph by Daniel Nicoletta.

Left: *After a verdict of voluntary manslaughter was announced in the Dan White trial rather than the anticipated verdict of murder, gays erupted in "White Night" riots. Later the same night, gays and police confronted each other on Castro Street, and a police rampage erupted at the Elephant Walk bar.*

sible for his actions because he had been bingeing on junk food and was on a "sugar high" at the time of the murders. Five thousand queers caused more than a million dollars in damage to public property during rioting that night, setting police cars on fire and trashing City Hall. SFPD officers retaliated by attacking the Elephant Walk, a gay bar in the Castro.

As the decade wound to a close, San Francisco's queer community found itself in a contradictory situation. Blatant homophobia and blasé acceptance of les-

Opposite Page: Sylvester's second Top 40 hit, "You Make Me Feel (Mighty Real)" (Blue Thumb Records), moved into the Top 40 on February 17, 1979, where it stayed for 36 weeks, peaking at number 3. Courtesy of GLC, SFPL.

Right: California State Liquor authorities closed down Fe-Be's, the four-year-old Folsom leather bar, on September 30, 1970, after reports that patrons were openly.having sex in the establishment. One of the bar's regulars said, "The place was notorious for its Sunday afternoons which were pure, unadulterated sex orgies. The whole back of the bar was transformed into a massive grope-a-torium where anything happened." Fe-Be's reopened in 1971 and became famous for, among other things, its two-foot-high promotional statue "The Fe-Be's Man" showing Michelangelo's David in leather pants, vest, and cap.

bians and gays stood side by side; militant activism coexisted with apolitical assimilationism. A week after 20,000 lesbians and gays turned out for "Gay Night" at Great America amusement park in May 1979, 1,500 men took to the streets in the Castro to protest the police posting anti-gay signs on public property. The city of Berkeley passed a comprehensive gay rights ordinance (including spousal benefits for domestic partners), but a federal appeals court ruled that lesbians and gays were not entitled to protection against employment discrimination. Lesbian mothers were beginning to win custody cases in Alameda County while San Francisco Mayor Dianne Feinstein was telling readers of the *Ladies Home Journal* that she sometimes found the "gay lifestyle" offensive. A decade that began in fiery street protests ended with queers dancing to "Disco Inferno" in clubs like the Trocadero Transfer. As the 1980s dawned, new troubles loomed on the horizon. Ronald Reagan, the Moral Majority, and other representatives of social forces generally hostile to queer people were well on their way to mainstream power. And another threat, serious enough in itself without a politically repressive climate to foster its growth, was already loose in the community.

Sylvester and the Hot Band

Photograph by Rick Gerharter/Impact Visuals.

The Plague Years:

LIVING IN THE AGE OF AIDS, 1980–1991

*H*ow does one even attempt to mark the beginning of a vastly complex phenomenon that has

been unfolding for more than 15 years, or bring an event of planetary proportions down to the local

level? How does one speak of the impact on a particular community of a force of nature that is

transforming the conditions under which the human species must struggle to exist—a force that

depopulates nations, exhausts health care resources, kills people before they breed, infects new life

with the promise of early death, contaminates pleasure with the fear of personal annihilation, and

haunts the living imagination as the starkest potential in our private and collective fates? How

does one possibly talk about the beginning of the AIDS epidemic in San Francisco?

Any number of discrete instances suggest themselves: The undatable moment in the late

1970s when a new pathogen was first transmitted to sexually active individuals in the Bay Area's

gay male population. The moment on November 25, 1980, when Ken Horne, the first PWA

(person with AIDS) reported to the Centers for Disease Control (CDC), stepped into Dr. James

Above: *AIDS activist Bobbi Campbell (left), the 16th San Franciscan to be diagnosed with the disease but the first to publically disclose his status, was featured on the cover of* Newsweek, *August 8, 1983. He died in 1984.* Photograph © by Cathy Cade.

Opposite page: *Flyers posted in the window of the old Star Pharmacy on Castro Street, describing "gay cancer," December 1981.* Photograph by Rink Foto.

Groundwater's office with Kaposi's sarcoma (KS) lesions and swollen lymph nodes. April 22, 1981—the day UCSF dermatologist Marcus Conant learned of Ken Horne's ailments, after hearing just the day before from a colleague in New York of several KS cases there among gay men, and began to wonder if some unknown infectious agent might be involved. Perhaps it was when people here read the AP wire story, first announced by the CDC in the *Morbidity and Mortality Weekly Report* June 5, 1981, of a curious cluster of pneumocistis carinii pneumonia (PCP) cases in Los Angeles—or a month later on July 4 when they learned of another *MMWR* report that detailed KS and PCP clusters in San Francisco, Los Angeles, and New York. Maybe it was the afternoon that Dr. Selma Dritz, an epidemiologist with the San Francisco Department of Public Health, started compiling information from the case-control study conducted here by the CDC that fall, when she drew the first epidemiological maps that linked the earliest known AIDS cases. Perhaps it was "KS Poster Boy" Bobbi Campbell's public discussion of his illness in of the *Sentinel* on December 10, 1981, or the flyers describing "gay cancer" he posted soon thereafter in the old Star Pharmacy window on Castro Street. While all of these instances called the epidemic to the attention of an ever-widening audience, none quite suffices as a moment of origin. Rather, each signaled an increasingly acute level of awareness that San Francisco's gay community had become one significant node in a global pandemic already well underway.

The emergence of AIDS cannot be reduced to any individual moment, however, because AIDS emerged from a context, not from an isolated event traceable to a single originating cause. Patterns of sexual activity that developed in—and were made possible by—the emergence of extensive gay male communities in major U.S. urban centers like New York, San Francisco, and Los Angeles created just one of the environments in which HIV could thrive. Bathhouses, bars, book-

stores, cruising grounds, and theaters helped foster situations where some men could meet and have sexual encounters with large numbers of other men. The susceptibility of San Francisco's gay male population to a malady like AIDS had long been evident in its high rate of sexually transmitted diseases (STDs) and gastrointestinal parasites. Gays made up 80 percent of the city's 70,000 annual VD clinic visits by the late 1970s, and since the 1960s had been targeted by public health workers as a population needing special attention and services. In addition to the permissive mores of the sexual revolution and gay liberation, another important factor contributing to the high incidence of STDs was the fact that—with the notable exception of hepatitis B—most diseases could be easily cured with readily available antibiotics. For many men, a few shots of penicillin seemed a small price to pay for the excitement of an adventurous sex life.

Although much remains to be learned about HIV infection and no cure for AIDS is yet in sight, after fifteen years of experience there is less confusion about the basic mechanisms through which the virus perpetuates itself—the passage of infected bodily fluids, especially blood and semen, through membranes or tears in

"An outbreak of a pneumonia strain usually restricted to infants, the elderly, and pregnant women has surfaced among young male adults in the city's gay community, according to the San Francisco Department of Public Health. At least five confirmed cases of gay men between the ages of 20 and 40 contracting the disease from the germ Pneumocistis Carinii have been reported in San Francisco hospitals," said Dr. Selma Dritz, assistant director of the city's Communicable Disease Control Office. Similar outbreaks of the rare pneumonia have been reported among gays in Los Angeles and on the East Coast. Dritz said the epidemic has baffled local, state, and federal health officials, who have no explanations on why the disease is being passed among homosexuals. "We have a couple of theories, but we are not prepared to speculate," Dritz said. "If we are wrong, it could start hysteria."

—First AP news service wire story on
AIDS in San Francisco,
June 5, 1981.

San Francisco's gay male population had been the target of a number of public health campaigns since the mid-1960s. Courtesy of GLHS.

the skin. Any activity that brings about this situation is a potential health risk. During the early days of the epidemic, however, fear and ignorance helped fuel a backlash against the radical sexual lifestyles that had taken shape in the wake of the gay liberation movement. The number of sexual partners, the type of sexual activity one engaged in, and recreational drug use habits—rather than specific acts that facilitated the transmission of the virus—were the principal topics of concern. While initial attention to these factors was based on their presence among the earliest known persons with AIDS at a time when virtually nothing was known about the disease, legitimate concerns quickly dovetailed with panicky reactions and moralistic condemnation. Bathhouses and sex clubs came to be seen by some as dangerous disease pits, responsible for the spread of the virus. Rancorous public hearings on the bathhouse issue in 1984 divided the gay men's community. Closure advocates sought to eradicate the places where risky activities transpired, while proponents of the bathhouses raised civil-liberties issues and argued that it would be better to use the clubs and baths to educate their patrons about the dangers of unsafe sex. The San Francisco Department of Public Health used its emergency powers to order the bathhouses closed on April 9, 1984.

Michel Foucault, the eminent French intellectual whose multi-volume work on the history of sexuality revolutionized that field of study, taught at UC Berkeley in the late 1970s and early 1980s before returning to Paris, where he died of AIDS in 1983. His experiences in urban queer communities in the United States informed his theoretical work. Foucault said, "You find emerging in places like San Francisco and New York what might be called laboratories of sexual experimentation."

89

July 15, 1983.

The Hothouse, San Francisco's legendary four-story, 10,000-square-foot bathhouse, closed its doors in the wake of growing concerns over the spread of AIDS.

Dr. Mervyn Silverman, director of the San Francisco Department of Public Health, holds a press conference to issue an order to close gay bathhouses, April 9, 1984.
Photograph by Rink Foto.

In spite of an early attempt by some medical researchers to label the new syndrome GRID—Gay-Related Immune Deficiency—HIV-related illnesses have never been the exclusive domain of gay men. Virtually an entire generation of hemophiliacs was destroyed by AIDS. Those infected through heterosexual intercourse, especially among intravenous drug users, now represent the fastest-growing segment of the HIV positive population. AIDS represents a much more serious threat to Africa and Asia than it does to the United States. Still, because of the early visibility of the disease among gays in the U.S., American gays and lesbians have played a critical role in the global fight against AIDS. Nowhere has this been truer than in San Francisco. Not only did the men's and women's communities here cooperate to an unprecedented degree, but a widely emulated model for providing AIDS services quickly took shape. Due to the entrenched presence of queers in the city's bureaucratic machinery and a long history of community organizing, San Francisco was prepared like no other place on earth to mount a response

Left: *Founded by Ruth Brinker, Project Open Hand delivers food to the homes of persons with AIDS.* Photograph by Rick Gerharter/Impact Visuals.

"We are People With AIDS . . . We feel that closure of bathhouses and private clubs is not the real issue; rather, the issue is the education of gay men as to what specific sexual practices involve the exchange of bodily fluids and thus are 'high-risk' for the transmission of AIDS, and to learn and practice low-risk 'safe-sex' techniques wherever and whenever they have sex . . . We feel that, unless the educational issue is addressed satisfactorily, that closing bathhouses and private clubs will not significantly reduce the incidence of AIDS and will not save lives . . . We who have AIDS [oppose] any attempt to close the baths and clubs as a shallow, cosmetic, dangerous, and ultimately ineffective symbolic gesture."

—Bobbi Campbell,
People With AIDS flyer,
April 2, 1984.

to the epidemic. A partnership coalesced between government and community-based organizations, and a relatively coordinated set of services for persons with AIDS soon developed, including education and prevention, testing, outpatient care, housing, counseling, and hospices. The first generation of AIDS service-providers—such as the San Francisco AIDS Foundation, the Shanti Project, the Haight-Ashbury Free Clinic, the AIDS Health Project, and the Pacific Center for Human Growth—has been joined by newer groups like Prevention Point, Project Open Hand, and the Tenderloin AIDS Resource Center, which formed in response to the constantly evolving course of the epidemic, as well as in response to the perceived shortcomings of existing services.

"*SF AIDS Model: A Tour of the Ruins.* San Francisco's response to the AIDS crisis is touted around the world as the model response to the epidemic. As inadequate as the city's response always was, today nearly all agree that the model is falling apart. Government inaction and lack of funding at all levels forced the creation of the so-called 'model' system of AIDS care, treatment, and education fueled by volunteers and private donations. Now all the volunteers are burning out, and they should never have been expected to provide the services to the PWAs in the first place. Moreover the 'model' is based on the racist, sexist, classist assumption that all people infected with HIV in San Francisco are white middle-class gay men, living in the Castro. While other communities impacted by the epidemic still wait for desperately needed services, the model built to serve gay white men crumbles."

—**Protest/tour sponsored by ACT-UP and Queerline Tours held in conjunction with the 6th International AIDS Conference, June 21, 1990.**

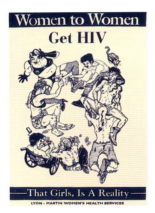

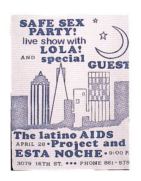

One of the biggest challenges in providing effective AIDS education is the need to develop materials that address the specific needs of a variety of target populations. Photographs courtesy of GLHS.

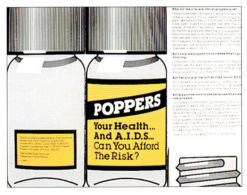

DON'T FUCK WITH A USER....

The San Francisco model relied largely on volunteer labor and charitable giving because public funds simply were not made available. Securing adequate funding for AIDS has been such a chronic problem that institutionalized homophobia is the only persuasive explanation. The Reagan administration in Washington embraced a policy of malignant neglect that conservative California Governor George Deukmejian was only too eager to follow. A few quick-witted gay state employees—like Stan Hadden in Senator Daniel Roberti's office and Levi Kammel in the Department of Public Health—had immediately grasped the threat posed by AIDS and by 1983 were quietly working behind the scenes to help direct millions of dollars in discretionary funds toward the community-based organizations and local government agencies best suited to deal with the public health emergency. But even when such funds became available, as when State Assembly Speaker Willie Brown rushed through approximately $3 million in emergency appropriations to the University of California system for medical research in 1983, policymakers and administrators were maddeningly slow to act—UC officials sat on the funds for half a year before distributing them to research scientists. In spite of such frustrations, UC campuses in the Bay Area have made crucial contributions to understanding the AIDS epidemic and providing health care services to people with AIDS. The UCSF medical

March 6, 1984.
....
A casting of George Segal's sculpture *Gay Liberation* placed at Stanford University was attacked and damaged by a hammer-wielding vandal. It was vandalized a second time by someone who spray-painted the word "AIDS" on it.

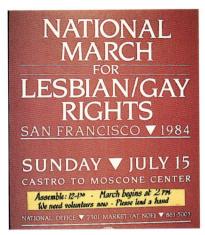

July 15, 1984. National March for Lesbian and Gay Rights advances down Market Street from the Castro to the Moscone Center, the day before the Democratic National Convention begins in San Francisco. Photograph by Rink Foto. Poster courtesy of GLHS.

center established the first KS clinic in 1981, and set up a special AIDS ward at San Francisco General, its teaching hospital, in 1983. Epidemiologists at Berkeley and UCSF conducted the first large-scale case-control study, and other scientists in the UC system were instrumental in developing and implementing the HIV anti-body test. In the private sector, Bay Area biotechnology companies like Genentech have been at the forefront of ongoing efforts to develop an AIDS vaccine.

By 1985, most of the current AIDS infrastructure was in place, and the implacable fact of AIDS was beginning to work its way into general public consciousness. The crisis was by no means over, but it had become a regular, ongoing feature of queer life rather than the emergency of the moment. In addition to donating countless volunteer hours attending to the needs of the sick, Bay Area queers began to turn more of their attention to the process of grieving and commemoration. The first AIDS candlelight memorial march had been held May 2, 1982, but it was not until 1986 that the Names Project Memorial Quilt, the best-known testament to people who have lost their lives in the AIDS epidemic, was begun by Cleve Jones. At the same time, Bay Area residents participated in actions designed to keep public attention focused on AIDS, and to assert pressure for more

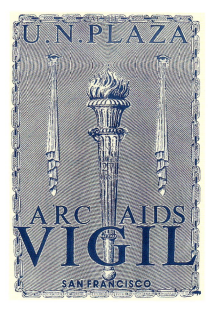

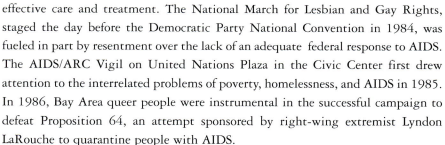

effective care and treatment. The National March for Lesbian and Gay Rights, staged the day before the Democratic Party National Convention in 1984, was fueled in part by resentment over the lack of an adequate federal response to AIDS. The AIDS/ARC Vigil on United Nations Plaza in the Civic Center first drew attention to the interrelated problems of poverty, homelessness, and AIDS in 1985. In 1986, Bay Area queer people were instrumental in the successful campaign to defeat Proposition 64, an attempt sponsored by right-wing extremist Lyndon LaRouche to quarantine people with AIDS.

One of the most important lessons of the AIDS epidemic has been that even amid grief, outrage, and a numbing death rate, the life of the community continues. The social, political, economic, and cultural trends that had been driving queer culture for decades did not come to a halt because of AIDS, however much they were transformed by its impact. Even as the epidemic was beginning its course, lesbians and gays were consolidating the inroads they had made into institutional politics during the 1970s—a process grotesquely distorted in the CBS documentary "Gay Power, Gay Politics," televised nationally on April 26, 1980. Mary Morgan became the first openly lesbian judge upon being appointed to the San Francisco Municipal Court in 1981. By 1983, local gays and lesbians had orga-

Left: *The Names Project AIDS Memorial Quilt on display in the Moscone Center. The quilt was begun in 1986 by Cleve Jones, who created the first panel to commemorate his best friend, Mark Feldman.* Photograph by Rink Foto.

Above: *Begun in 1985, the AIDS/ARC Vigil on United Nations Plaza in the Civic Center has drawn attention to the interconnections between homelessness, poverty, and HIV illnesses.* Poster design by Ron Henggeler. Courtesy of GLHS.

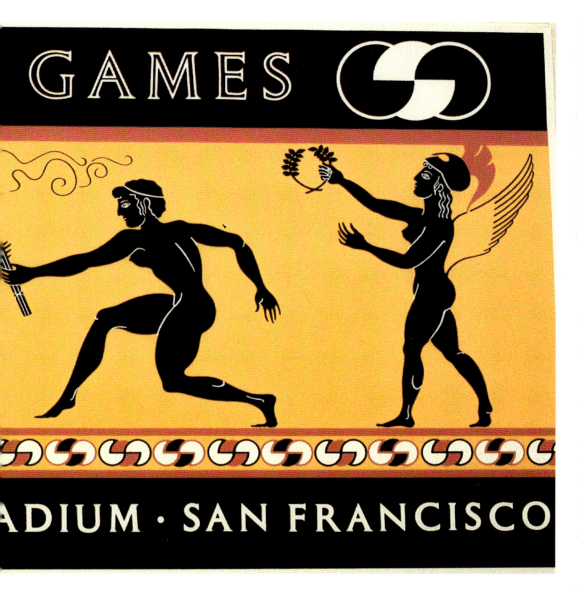

GAMES

ADIUM · SAN FRANCISCO

The first Gay Games were held at Kezar Stadium August 28 to September 5, 1982, with 1,300 male and female athletes participating in 16 sports. The games were originally called the Gay Olympics until a successful lawsuit by the U.S. Olympic Committee forced a change of name. Dr. Tom Waddell conceived of the Games as a way to counter stereotypes of lesbians and gays and to overcome the divisiveness he saw in the queer community: "The most important thing about the Games is the destruction of 'isms' like ageism, sexism, and racism." The week-long series of competitions was so successful it was repeated four years later in San Francisco, followed by Gay Games III in Vancouver in 1990 and Gay Games IV in New York in 1994. After Dr. Waddell died of AIDS in July 1987, a medical clinic in the Tenderloin was named in his honor. Photograph by Rink Foto. Poster courtesy of GLHS.

November 1981.
Atlas Savings and Loan, the nation's
first gay-owned bank, opened at
Market and 14th streets.

From 1981 to 1985.
Arthur Lazere, active for many years
in the Golden Gate Business
Association, wrote a nationally syndi-
cated column called "On the Job:
Gay People at Work."

April 22, 1982.
A federal judge in San Francisco
ruled that the Immigration and
Naturalization Service may not bar
entry to foreign visitors solely because
they are gay. The INS had tried to
prohibit Carl Hill, a British journalist,
from entering the U.S. at San
Francisco International Airport on the
grounds that his homosexuality constituted a "psychopathic personality."

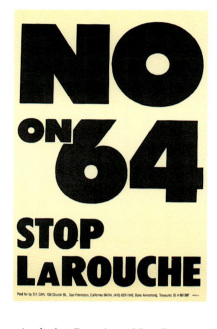

nized the Bay Area Non-Partisan Alliance, California's largest queer political action committee. In contrast to San Jose, Davis, and Santa Clara County—where gay rights ordinances had failed early in the decade—Berkeley instituted the nation's first spousal benefits package for lesbian and gay city employees on December 5, 1984. In San Francisco, Harry Britt had filled Harvey Milk's seat at City Hall, while Tom Ammiano, Pat Norman, Roberta Achtenberg, and Carole Migden all began their public careers in a variety of electoral contests—culminating in 1990's "Lavender Sweep" in the Board of Supervisors race.

The women's culture that took shape in the 1970s continued to thrive in the new decade. Mama Bear's Bookstore and Coffee House, A Woman's Place for Books, Ollie's Bar (with its large meeting room, Radclyffe Hall), and the Brick Hut Cafe all provided gathering places for queer women in the East Bay. In San Francisco, lesbians and bisexual women played a significant role in developing the Valencia Street corridor—the city's new queer enclave in the Mission District. Anchored by Old Wives' Tales Bookstore in 1976, the Artemis Cafe in 1977 and the Women's Building in 1979, other women-oriented businesses followed, and by the early 1980s a vital neighborhood had taken shape. Rikki Streicher opened

Above: *By the early 1980s, the Valencia Street corridor bustled with activities of interest to the women's community.* Courtesy of GLHS.

Right: *Opening night at the Artemis Cafe, 1977.* Photograph © by Cathy Cade.

1980.
....
Bay Area Career Women, the largest lesbian organization in the United States, was founded by Nicole Shapiro.

Amelia's, a lesbian bar that rivaled Maud's in popularity. The Women's Press Project offered on-the-job training by doing printing and publishing work for members of the queer and feminist communities. Osento's Japanese-style bathhouse provided women with a sensual treat, while Good Vibrations—the sex-toy store that built a national following by advertising its mail-order services in the pages of the pioneering sex-positive magazine *On Our Backs*—helped cultivate a newly adventurous lesbian sexuality. Modern Times Bookstore, a neighborhood fixture neither specifically queer nor primarily woman-oriented, owed much of its success to the vision and hard work of such gay and lesbian community leaders as Tede Mathews, Ruth Mahaney, and Amber Hollibaugh. At the hub of the Valencia Street scene was the Valencia Rose, which served as an unofficial community center during much of the 1980s. The club provided space for informal socializing as well as political and organizational meetings, and became an important venue for emerging lesbian and gay performers—as well as for Whoopi Goldberg, who played repeatedly at the Bay Area's premier queer cabaret early in her career. The

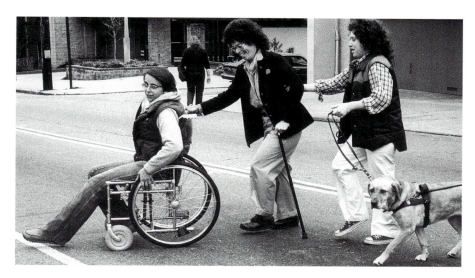

Left: *Members of the Lesbians with Disabilities Support Group, 1982.* Photograph © by Cathy Cade.

Valencia Rose is perhaps best remembered for its weekly gay comedy night, where such future stars as Marga Gomez and Lea DeLaria got their starts.

Artistic and cultural life in the Bay Area's queer community reached a new level of sophistication during the 1980s. Dorothy Allison's 1988 collection of short stories, *Trash,* paved the way for her later success with *Bastard Out of Carolina.* Acclaimed British expatriate poet Thom Gunn, who had lived in San Francisco with college sweetheart Mike Kitay since the 1950s, began to turn his considerable talents toward expressing the deep emotions associated with the AIDS epidemic. The Lesbian and Gay Film Festival developed into an important international event during this period under the guidance of Michael Lumpkin. Originally a venue for experimental short works, the festival moved to the Castro Theater in 1981 and expanded its two-day program to include a week's worth of feature films and gala celebrations. Before the decade closed, the film festival regularly premiered important new work by such notable filmmakers as Gus Van Sant and Pedro Almodovar. In 1985, Bill Walker and a handful of other women and men with an eye toward the future organized the Gay and Lesbian Historical Society of Northern California. Working as a nurse on the AIDS ward at San Francisco General Hospital convinced Walker that if an effort to collect and preserve the fragile records of the remarkably rich queer culture in the Bay Area were not begun immediately, vital information about our collective past would be irretrievably lost.

Above: *Founded by Debbi Sundahl in 1984,* On Our Backs *started a new trend in sex-positive reading for women. Over the years, the magazine has been edited by "Susie Sexpert" Bright; Marcy Shiner, who went on to edit some of the popular* Herotica *collections;* Girlfriends *founding editor Heather Findlay; and Bayla Travis. Sundahl, who later began* Fatale Videos, *sold* On Our Backs *to Melissa Murphy in 1994.* Courtesy of GLHS.

1982.
....
Onyx, the first black lesbian newsletter, began publishing. It was produced by a Berkeley African-American lesbian collective to promote a variety of anti-racist activities.

DE LARIA

RAGING BULL

In the early 1980s, the Valencia Rose helped advance the career of many future celebrities. Impresario Donald Montwill, who booked many of the acts, continued to promote queer talent such as Lea De Laria (top) and Marga Gomez (right) at Josie's Cabaret and Juice Joint in the 1990s.

Opposite Page: *Maud's Study, Rikki Streicher's immensely popular lesbian bar, closed September 15, 1989.* Last Call at Maud's, *a 1993 documentary by Paris Poirier, captured this historic moment on film and also chronicled the role of the world's longest-running lesbian bar in the life of the city. Streicher was an early and influential member of the Tavern Guild who remained prominent in business affairs until shortly before her death from breast cancer in 1994.* Photograph by Rink Foto.

102

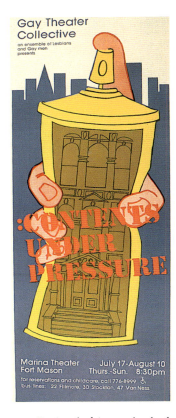

When Gloria Anzáldúa and Cherrié Moraga, two Latina lesbians who had taken up residence in Northern California, published their anthology *This Bridge Called My Back: Writings by Radical Women of Color* in 1981, they announced one of the dominant themes of the decade—attention to racial and ethnic diversity. By the 1980s, the Bay Area had become the most racially diverse area in the United States and had supported a history of activism around multicultural diversity stretching back at least to the Third World Student Strike at San Francisco State in 1968. The queer community reflected this broader pattern, and several queers of color were at the forefront of the movement for multicultural higher education—of necessity thinking more rigorously about the intersections of race, class,

Left: *Nellie Wong, Kitty Tsui, and Merle Woo, members of the poetry and performance collective Unbound Feet Three, 1981.*
Photograph © by Cathy Cade.

March 15, 1985.

A group of activist scholars, some of whom had been associated with the San Francisco Lesbian and Gay History Project, founded the San Francisco Bay Area Gay and Lesbian Historical Society to create a permanent archives documenting local queer history. The group later changed its name to the Gay and Lesbian Historical Society of Northern California.

Right: *Michael J. Smith founded Black and White Men Together in 1980. He also published* Quarterly, *an articulate and assertive periodical devoted to promoting the interests of lesbians and gays of color. In 1983, he issued* Colorful People and Places, *the most comprehensive resource guide then available for queer people of color, and still an important source of historical information.* Courtesy of Russell Smith Photography and GLHS.

gender, and sexual orientation than many others were habitually called upon to do. One of the early battles in the struggle for multicultural education involved the politically motivated series of dismissals and rehirings during the early 1980s of Merle Woo, a Chinese-American lesbian socialist teaching ethnic studies at the University of California at Berkeley. Woo eventually left UC for the CSU system, where she continued to be an effective educator.

In spite of a growing awareness of complex "hybrid" identities, racial biases that usually remained unstated kept issues of color in the background within the organized queer community. Queer groups addressing issues of color began to appear in the mid-1970s, but this trend accelerated rapidly in the 1980s. Black and White Men Together formed in 1980, and the Association of Lesbian/Gay Asians formed in 1981, to mention only two examples. A Little More—a women's dance club with a primarily black, Latina, and Filipina clientele—was located in the Mission near Esta Noche, a Latino men's bar with a strong drag presence. Berry's, a long-established bar in Oakland, served mostly black male patrons. By the decade's close, various queers-of-color groups were producing a substantial body of newsletters and periodicals. The Gay Asian-Pacific Alliance—originating in a men's support group at the Pacific Center in 1988—published *Lavender Godzilla. Trikone* focused on the South Asian community, and *Aché* was aimed at women of African-American descent.

Bisexuals and transgendered people also began moving from the margins to the center of Bay Area's organized queer community in the 1980s. Dr. Maggi Rubenstein, who had helped found the San Francisco Sex Information Switchboard in 1972 and served as Dean of Students at the Institute for the Advanced Study of Human Sexuality, had been a bisexual activist in the Bay Area since the mid-

BLACK & WHITE
MEN TOGETHER

Write :

BWMT-
279 Collingwood
San Francisco CA 94114

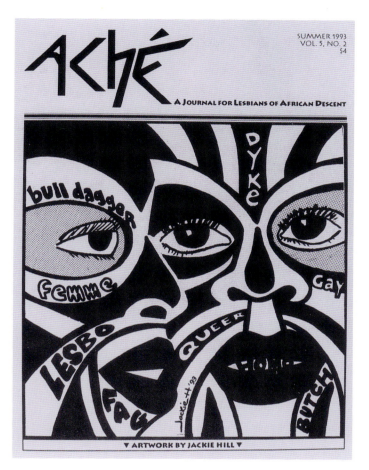

ACHÉ

SUMMER 1993
VOL. 5, NO. 2
$4

A JOURNAL FOR LESBIANS OF AFRICAN DESCENT

▼ ARTWORK BY JACKIE HILL ▼

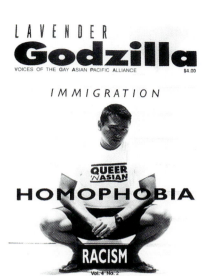

LAVENDER
Godzilla
VOICES OF THE GAY ASIAN PACIFIC ALLIANCE $4.00

IMMIGRATION

QUEER 'N ASIAN

HOMOPHOBIA

RACISM

Vol. 4 No. 2

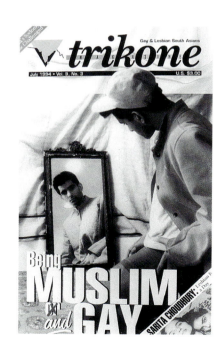

trikone
Gay & Lesbian South Asians

July 1994 • Vol. 9, No. 3   U.S. $3.00

Being
MUSLIM
and GAY

SARITA CHOUDHURY

The titles of newsletters produced by ethnic and racial groups within the queer community often reflect the self-image these groups want to express. "Aché" is a Yoruban Nigerian word that means both a blessing bestowed upon another and the force or power that gives one life. "Trikone" is from the Sanskrit for triangle, suggesting the ancient roots of South Asian queer identities, as well as involvement in the contemporary international lesbian and gay community whose symbol recuperates the one used to mark Nazi concentration camp prisoners. Lavender Godzilla *makes a flaming queen of the powerful cross-cultural icon, a playfully monstrous Asian-American figure that reworks traditional dragon imagery for the fractured mindframes of the atomic age.* Aché *cover art by Jackie Hill.* Trikone *cover photo by Jackie Wey.* Lavender Godzilla *cover by George Choy. Photographs courtesy of GLHS.*

June 17, 1989.

Black lesbian poet and activist Pat Parker died in Oakland. A Houston native involved with the Black Panther Party in the 1960s, Parker moved to the Bay Area in 1971, where she helped develop the Women's Press Collective. As medical services coordinator of the Oakland Feminist Women's Health Center from 1978 to 1987, Parker oversaw the clinic's expansion from one site to six, and introduced new services such as second-trimester abortions and a sperm bank. Her signature volume of poems, *Movements in Black,* was first published in 1978.

Dance for older lesbians sponsored by GLOE (Gay and Lesbian Outreach to Elders) in 1985. Photograph © by Cathy Cade.

Lani Kaahumanu (left) *and other members of the Bay Area bisexual community march in the 1985 Freedom Day Parade.* Photograph © by Cathy Cade.

1960s. She founded the now-defunct Bisexual Center in 1976, but only in the late 1980s, with the organization of the Bay Area Bisexual Network (BABN) and BiPol, a political action committee, did the issue of bisexuality gain widespread visibility in the "monosexual" queer community. *Bi Any Other Name,* a pathbreaking anthology coedited by local bi activist Lani Kaahumanu, appeared in 1991. The transgender community became more organized in the 1980s, too. Peer support groups continued to operate out of the Pacific Center for Human Growth in Berkeley, as they had done since the 1970s. In San Francisco, the Center for Special Problems provided the bulk of social services for the city's transgender population, and Dr. Paul Walker operated the Janus Information Facility, a clearinghouse on information about transvestism and transsexuality. One of the most striking developments of the decade, however, was the extent to which transgendered people who had not found niches for themselves in the gay drag or butch lesbian subcultures began to break out of the rigid medical and psychiatric models that labeled their desires diseases, and to organize themselves socially. Founded in 1982, the Educational TV Channel, whose membership is made up largely of male-to-female transvestites, is now the largest organization for cross-dressers and

Leather and S/M in the 1980s

In spite of leathermen being scapegoated in some quarters as irresponsible agents of the AIDS epidemic, and leatherdykes being labeled anti-feminist by women who didn't share their sexual tastes, San Francisco's S/M and fetish scene flourished in the 1980s. Although many popular bars closed as a result of the epidemic, the leather community inaugurated an important new institution in 1984—the Folsom Street Fair. This annual event has become the second-largest yearly queer gathering in the nation, exceeded only by the San Francisco Freedom Day parade. The formation of the women's S/M scene was accelerated by the organization of the Outcasts in 1985. By 1986, the women's leather community had matured enought to sponsor the first International Ms. Leather Competition. The Society of Janus continued to be an initial point of contact for many people seeking to explore a leather lifestyle. Mr. Marcus, "the Herb Caen of Leatherworld," has been keeping tabs on the S/M community for many years in his regular column in the *BAR*.

LINKS Courtesy of GLHS.

Folsom Street Fair. Photograph by Rick Gerharter/Impact Visuals.

Growing Pains. Courtesy of GLHS.

SAMOIS PRESENTS
The First Annual Leather Dance and Ms. Leather Contest

Sleazy dance music by DJ Gayle Rubin

$4/$3 if you're wearing leather

Saturday, Sept. 5, 9:00 pm
Radclyffe Hall
Ollie's, 4130 Telegraph
Oakland 653-6017

Contest registrations accepted until 10:00 pm
Proceeds to benefit publication of **COMING TO POWER**

Growing Pains

December, 1981

Happy Holidays!

110

May 5, 1987.

The 21st Street Baths, San Francisco's last gay bathhouse, closed its doors.

September 9, 1987.

James Short was awarded more than $2 million by a San Francisco jury after he broke up with his lover of 19 years, in what is considered the first gay palimony case.

"Is it possible that the United States government has initiated biological warfare against the lesbian and gay community, Africans, other people of color, and drug users? Reports have been circulating worldwide since 1982 that AIDS was a creation of our own government's Biochemical Warfare Program."
—"AIDS: Smallpox-Infected Blankets in 1980s Drag?"
Grassroots AIDS Information Network/COUNTERPROBE pamphlet, circa 1987. Courtesy of GLHS.

"Women's liberation and gay liberation [are] part of the same thing: a weakening of moral standards of this nation. It is appalling to see parades in San Francisco and elsewhere claiming 'gay pride' and all that. What in the world do they have to be proud of?"

—Nancy Reagan,
The Boston Globe, **March 31, 1981.**

other transgendered people on the West Coast. In 1986, Lou Sullivan established FTM, one of the earliest organizations devoted exclusively to female-to-male cross-dressers and transsexuals.

The growth and increasing complexity of the Bay Area's queer community during the 1980s took place against a backdrop of increasing right-wing hostility towards what the conservatives euphemistically referred to as "alternative lifestyles." In 1988, Southern California U.S. Representative William Dannemyer sponsored the implicitly anti-gay Proposition 102, which if passed would have

required mandatory reporting of HIV-positive individuals to state authorities. In suburban Concord, east of San Francisco, voters repealed a gay rights ordinance in 1989. Rather than simply respond to the newly aggressive tactics of the Traditional Values Coalition and other Christian fundamentalists, however, queers also became more militant. The AIDS Action Coalition, organized in 1987, was one of the first groups to reflect this new sensibility. By late 1988, the Coalition had spun off into a new group—ACT-UP/SF. The "AIDS Coalition to Unleash Power" was part of a national network that also included loosely affiliated chapters

Militant AIDS activists protest at the offices of pharmaceuticals giant Burroughs-Wellcome, makers of AZT, whom they accused of profiteering. Photograph by Rick Gerharter/Impact Visuals.

June 26, 1988.

Art Agnos became the first San Francisco mayor to ride in one of the city's Gay Pride parades.

March 1988.

Straight students threw tomatoes at a group of gays and lesbians at UC Berkeley's Gay/Lesbian/Bisexual Awareness week.

"As people living with AIDS we ask you: Are you sick and tired of being stuck on this bridge? So are we! Are you wondering how long it will be? So are we! Are you wondering why me? So are we! Many of us have AIDS or AIDS Related Complex (ARC). Many of us have tested HIV positive. We are gay men and lesbians who see our community being devastated by the AIDS epidemic. We are straight and bisexual people who are involved in the fight against AIDS. We are here for countless others who were too sick to come and for tens of thousands around the world who are dead. AIDS has been forced into the center of all of our lives. We are here each one of us as people living with AIDS."
—From the flyer passed out by Stop AIDS Now Or Else (SANOE), an ad hoc coalition of AIDS activists, on the Jan 31, 1989, Golden Gate Bridge closure. Photograph by Rick Gerharter/Impact Visuals.

I Stopped on the Bridge to Stop AIDS
Courtesy of GLHS.

in New York, Los Angeles, and elsewhere. Besides engaging in acts of civil disobedience on AIDS-related issues, ACT-UP participated in a number of other progressive causes like abortion rights and the anti-racist movement.

A slow-burning sense of outrage and a deepening cynicism about the quality of life in late-20th-century America undergirded the protests of the militant AIDS groups. When George Bush was elected president in 1988, it signaled the continuation of policies that many queer people found murderous. At the same time, a nationwide recession hit California's economy particularly hard, producing a double-digit unemployment rate. Government services were being slashed at precisely the moment when they were most needed. While the Berlin Wall came down in Europe and Mikhail Gorbachev transformed the Soviet Union, the United States seemed to become even more deeply entrenched in the reactionary social climate that had followed the upheavals of the late 1960s. As the new decade began—the last decade of the millennium—many Bay Area residents seemed to be quietly taking stock of lives that seemed increasingly untenable, and to be testing creative new strategies for resisting the most deadening aspects of the dominant culture. Out of the depths of this anger and frustration, a new movement—the queer movement—announced itself with a vengeance.

October 6, 1989.
158 SFPD officers violently attacked a peaceful AIDS demonstration organized by ACT NOW and subsequently placed four square blocks of the Castro neighborhood under house arrest for nearly an hour. Local artists publicized the "Night of Resistance" by designing red-splattered T-shirts overprinted with the words, "My domestic partner went to the Castro and all I got was this bloody T-shirt."

December 5, 1990.
Playwright Robert Chesley, a pioneer of AIDS theater, died in San Francisco. His debut work, *Hell, I Love You,* premiered at Theatre Rhinoceros in 1981. His later and better-known plays included *Night Sweat* and *Jerker,* whose full subtitle *(Or, The Helping Hand: A Pornographic Elegy with Redeeming Social Value and a Hymn to the Queer Men of San Francisco in Twenty Phone Calls, Many of Them Dirty)* suggests the tenor of his work.

Photograph by Rick Gerharter/Impact Visuals.

116

The Queer Here and Now, 1990—1995

*I*f 1991 was the "Year of the Queer," then New Year's Day dawned on January 16, the morning after U.S. bombs began falling on Iraq to usher in George Bush's "New World Order." A massive demonstration against the war converged on the Federal Building in San Francisco, making business as usual impossible in the Civic Center throughout the day. Before nightfall, the mass of protesters had swept through the streets to blockade the Pacific Stock Exchange before surging onto the Bay Bridge and closing it to vehicular traffic. Over the next several days, protesters throughout the Bay Area repeatedly took the freeways for brief moments, visiting upon American oil consumers a small taste of the disruptions of daily life wrought by war. Over the following weekend, so many people turned out for another massive protest in San Francisco that before even half the crowd had left the Dolores Park staging area, Civic Center Plaza was already swollen past capacity with protesters pouring in from the march down Market Street. And unlike the protests of the Vietnam War era, where gay liberationists remained largely invisible within the larger movement, queers were the most vital and visible faction of the short-lived coalition against the Gulf War.

Queer people were highly visible participants in the massive protests against the Persian Gulf War, January 1991. Photographs © by Cathy Cade (above) and Alyson Belcher (right).

The emergence of queer identities, sensibilities, and politics was not just the latest fad in the lesbian and gay community. It represented an ideological and generational shift as profound as the transition from a homophile mentality to gay liberation. It has been partly a youthful reinvention of established ways of differing from heterosexual norms, perpetuating lesbian and gay culture through its transformation. But it also represents a significant departure—an anti-identity rather than an identity. As a consequence of the diversity controversies of the 1980s and the multifaceted reactions against "political correctness," it became much easier to affirm what one wasn't (straight or racist, for example) rather than what one was. There's no better illustration of the complexities of postmodern queer identity issues than the convoluted self-statements that characterize contemporary

"I hate having to convince straight people that lesbians and gays live in a war zone, that we're surrounded by bomb blasts only we seem to hear, that our bodies and souls are heaped up high, dead from fright or bashed or raped, dying of grief or disease, stripped of our personhood. I hate straight people who can't listen to queer anger without saying 'Hey, all straight people aren't like that. I'm straight too, you know,' as if their egos don't get enough stroking or protection in this arrogant, heterosex-ist world. Why must we take care of them, in the midst of our just anger brought on by their fucked up soci-ety?! Why add the reassurance of 'Of course, I don't mean you. You don't act that way.' Let them figure out for themselves whether they deserve to be included in our anger. But of course, that would mean listening to our anger, which they almost never do."

—June 1990, "I Hate Straights," anonymously written early queer manifesto that originated in New York, but circulated in San Francisco as well.

"We use a range of non-violent tactics that extend beyond the tradition of 'go out, sit down, and get arrested' civil disobedience. Our approach works more with intellectual subversion and visual intervention, seizing and manipulating the territories of advertising and media, expanding the possibilities of technologies like xerox and fax, all with the assumption of no budget, with an emphasis on individual and local autonomy, and with plenty of hooligan energy. To some extent we draw on the basic motivation of adolescent rebellion: a grass-roots, in-your-face urge to say 'You think you're the authority? Well fuck off, I'm running my own life.'"

—Boy/Girl With Arms Akimbo, a San Francisco—based network of anonymous cultural activists, founded July 1989.
Courtesy of GLHS.

à kim´ bō, *a.* and *adv.* [ME: *in kenebowe*, lit., in keen bow, i.e. in a sharp curve; a folk etym. from ON: *keng-boginn*, bow bent] **1:** with hands on hips and elbows turned outwards, as in a stance of defiance. **2:** set in a bent position. **3:** held at an odd angle. **4:** having to do with cultural activism or visual intervention in an urban setting (e.g., *Girl with Arms ~*; *Boy with Arms ~*).

à kim´ bō, *a.* and *adv.* [ME: *in kenebowe*, lit., in keen bow, i.e. in a sharp curve; a folk etym. from ON: *keng-boginn*, bow bent] **1:** with hands on hips and elbows turned outwards, as in a stance of defiance. **2:** set in a bent position. **3:** held at an odd angle. **4:** having to do with cultural activism or visual intervention in an urban setting (e.g., *Girl with Arms ~*; *Boy with Arms ~*).

personals ads—"SWF, pagan, vegetarian, femme-of-center, lesbian identified but has sex w/ GM friends, nonsmoker, moderate drinker, into light spanking, seeks same for non-monogamous LTR." It became virtually impossible by the early 1990s to derive any kind of political position or social practice solely from the specificities of one's particular needs and kinks. Queerness was not about carving out a culturally sanctioned niche for a carefully crafted minority identity. Rather, it involved the perception of sharing space with people quite different from oneself who were nonetheless adversely affected by the same power structures. And perhaps this is why queers were so visible in the Persian Gulf War protests—the war clearly articulated a position many queers could define themselves against, one that allowed them to mobilize the oppositional affinities they shared with other protesters without compelling them to ground their actions in a common identity.

The queer movement has come to be associated with the 1990s, but its roots lie in the preceding decade. In San Francisco, the media-savvy style of activism associated with queerness in its political heyday crystallized in the work of Arms Akimbo, a collective of cultural activists who applied to a hostile mainstream society the harsh strategies queer people had learned from their engagements with the HIV virus—acknowledging, in effect, that the dominant culture's body seeks to eliminate us but that we can use its own means of resisting infection and reproducing itself to subvert its assault on our existence. Active in 1989 and 1990, Arms Akimbo earned a reputation for conceptually brilliant actions like "Art Attack II," staged during the controversy over NEA funding cuts for art deemed pornographic by the likes of Jesse Helms. Art Attack created its own "federal support" for the arts by wheat-pasting large posters of photographs by Robert Mapplethorpe and other controversial artist to the granite pillars of the Federal Building in San Francisco. Meanwhile, across the continent, AIDS activists in New York were just beginning to use the word "queer" in its current positive sense to mark what they considered to be radical political differences with older and more ineffective styles of activism. Their ideological counterparts in San Francisco were quick to follow suit, and "queer" became a buzzword nationwide.

Queer Nation—arguably the most important of the new groups to adopt the visually spectacular in-your-face tactics honed in the fight against AIDS—founded its San Francisco chapter on July 18, 1990, almost immediately after the organi-

"Being queer means leading a different sort of life. It's not about the mainstream, profit-margins, patriotism, patriarchy, or being assimilated. It's not about executive directors, privilege, and elitism. It's about being on the margins, defining ourselves; it's about gender-fuck and secrets, what's beneath the belt and deep inside the heart; it's about the night. Being queer is "grass roots" because we know that every one of us, every body, every cunt, every heart, every ass and dick is a world of pleasure waiting to be explored . . . Every time we fuck, we win."

—"Queers Read This!"
a rant "published anonymously by queers" in
tabloid form during the summer of 1990.

121

"We are Queer Nation. We are here to promote unity between all people—some of whom are like us, most of whom are not. We do not necessarily expect to understand the differences between our cultures, our desires, our beliefs, but we do seek to increase respect and acceptance for all our differences so that we may move into the twenty-first century with joy and dignity. Queer Nation is an informal, multicultural, direct action group committed to the recognition, preservation, expansion, and celebration of queer culture in all its diversity. We are dedicated to confronting society's bigotry, discrimination, violence, and misinformation."

—Queer Nation flyer,
July 1990.

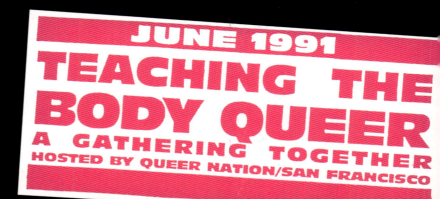

"The name of your new organization is INSULTING! . . . How such an ugly, demeaning name could have been chosen for an organization with such obviously well-intentioned, far-reaching goals is beyond me. I implore you, don't undo what other Gays and Lesbians have fought for, for so long!

—Ray Leland Caley,
the *Sentinel*, August 16, 1990;
first known letter to the editor in the Bay Area
press protesting use of the word "queer"
in a positive sense.

Left: *The trip by Queer Nation's Suburban Homosexual Outreach Project (SHOP) to Sun Valley Mall in Concord in 1990 angered some Contra Costa County lesbian and gay activists who felt their counterparts in the big city acted inappropriately, but the SHOP action nevertheless exemplified the in-your-face tactics of Queer Nation.* Photograph by Paul Miller, *Oakland Tribune.*

Queer Nation crack-n-peel stickers courtesy of GLHS.

Above: *"Mac," a participant in the First Annual San Francisco Drag King Competition, San Francisco Eagle, 1994.* Photograph by Daniel Nicoletta.

Right: *Justin Bond and Elvis Herselvis at the Castro Street Fair.* Photograph by Daniel Nicoletta.

zation of the original group in New York. In six remarkable months, Queer Nation conducted over 40 actions, like the kiss-in at the Powell Street cable car turn-around, the retro-chic Queer Be-In at Aquatic Park, and—as part of its Suburban Homosexual Outreach Project (SHOP)—several trips to Bay Area malls, where they staged scenes of everyday urban queer life for gaping audiences unaccustomed to such sights. Queer Nation also spawned several other groups of varying longevity, including LABIA (Lesbians and Bisexuals in Action) and the Castro Street Patrol. By 1992, the energy that made Queer Nation such a transformative force in contemporary society had flung it apart, but the existence of the group and the

tendencies it represented seem destined to mark a watershed in the history of sexuality in the United States. One indication of the pervasive influence of the queer movement of the early 1990s is the extent to which the word "queer" has lost much of its earlier pejorative force, as well as much of the specific political connotations that it carried at the beginning of the decade. It has come to stand for the wide range of marginalized sexual identities, practices, and communities sometimes excluded by the words "lesbian" and "gay," yet which also lie beyond the pale of normative society and share a rich history with homosexuality as it is currently understood.

Opening night at the Liquid Eyeliner exhibit, curated by D-L Alvarez, 1992. Left to right: *Brie Burkett, Laura Duran, Kimo, Jamie.* Photograph by Daniel Nicoletta.

Above: *February 13, 1994. In a rare moment of transsexual/drag cooperation, Transgender Nation and the Sisters of Perpetual Indulgence joined forces to protest transphobia at the downtown San Francisco Nordstrom's department store.* Photograph by Daniel Nicoletta.

The shifting status of transgender identities and practices in the contemporary gay and lesbian community illustrates the kind of realignments effected under the "queer" rubric. Drag has been enjoying a remarkable renaissance that has catapulted it out of the queer subculture into the mainstream mass media, fine arts, and high fashion, while the resurgence of butch and femme among younger lesbians has self-consciously reclaimed and reinterpreted a long-neglected aspect of pre-liberation working-class lesbian culture. Some of the old divisions between drags, butches, transsexuals, and transvestites began to break down in San Francisco in the early 1990s, melding into a provocative "transgender style" with a distinctive Bay Area flavor. Transsexual lesbian playwright Kate Bornstein's book *Gender Outlaw* and the photography of Daniel Nicoletta and Loren Cameron all reflect this sensibility, as do local music personalities Veronica Klaus, Elvis Herselvis, Justin Bond, and Minnie Pearl Necklace. The ambiance of Jordy Jones and Stafford's Club Confidential; the aesthetic choices made by curator and artist

D-L Alvarez in the 1990 *Liquid Eyeliner* exhibit; the sartorial sophistication demonstrated by participants in the 1994 drag king competition at the Eagle; and the attitudes and opinions voiced by the many contributors to *TNT: The Transsexual News Telegraph* embody this style as well.

Transsexuals in particular quickly seized the political opportunities they saw in the midst of these boundary-collapses within queer culture. Transgender Nation (TN), initially a focus group of Queer Nation that took on a life of its own when the parent group folded, was organized by male-to-female (MTF) transsexual Anne Ogborn in 1992. Besides calling attention to transphobic attitudes in the lesbian and gay community, TN also staged a protest at the 1993 meeting of the American Psychiatric Association (APA) at the Moscone Center. TN expressed its opposition to the labeling of transsexuality as an emotional disorder, just as the gay lib invasion of the APA in 1970 had opposed the similar pathologization of homosexuality.

Stafford, Jordy Jones, and Miss Kitty at the public hearing on transgender discrimination that culminated in a historic piece of transgender rights law, May 12, 1994.
Photograph by Rick Gerharter/Impact Visuals.

Under the direction of Cathy Jones, TN successfully lobbied for inclusion of the word "transgender" in the ever-lengthening title of the Freedom Day Parade in 1995. Less visible but more sustained transgender activism resulted in a landmark city ordinance prohibiting discrimination against transgendered individuals, which was signed into law in January 1995, making San Francisco only the fourth city in the nation to extend such protection. MTF transsexual Kiki Whitlock worked extensively with Larry Brinkin of the Lesbian/Gay/Bisexual (and now Transgender) Task Force of the San Francisco Human Rights Commission to convene a public hearing on transgender discrimination at City Hall on May 12, 1994. FTM community leader James Green edited the hours of testimony and hundreds of pages of reports into a usable document, whose findings formed the basis of the transgender antidiscrimination ordinance.

The Bay Area has come to support a burgeoning number of academic programs devoted to queer studies. A remarkable network of queer scholars has emerged both within and outside of the universities, built upon foundations laid in the 1970s by Jack Collins, John De Cecco, and members of the Gay Academic

Arthur Dong's (right) documentary Coming Out Under Fire, *based on Allan Bérubé's groundbreaking book about lesbians and gays in the military during World War II, premiered at the Castro Theater on March 10, 1994.* Photograph by Rink Foto.

Queer Higher Education

". . . We have been in the midst of a celebration . . . of the phantasmatic subject, the one who determines its world unilaterally, and which is in some measure typified by the looming heads of retired generals framed against the map of the Middle East, where the speaking head of this subject is shown the same size or larger than the area it seeks to dominate. This is, in a sense, the graphics of the imperialist subject, a visual allegory of the action itself . . . The subject is constructed through acts of differentiation that distinguish the subject from its constitutive outside, a domain of abjected alterity conventionally associated with the feminine, but clearly not exclusively. Precisely in this war we saw 'the Arab' figured as the abjected other as well as a site of homophobic fantasy made clear in the abundance of bad jokes grounded in the linguistic sliding from Saddam to Sodom."

—Judith Butler, feminist philosopher teaching at UC Berkeley since 1992 whose work has been closely identified with "queer theory," discussing the Persian Gulf War.

Queer theory became one of the fastest growing fields in academics following publication in 1992 of a special issue of the journal *differences* devoted to that topic, edited by UC Santa Cruz humanities professor Teresa de Lauretis. The leading journal for queer scholarship is now *GLQ: A Journal of Lesbian and Gay Studies,* cofounded and coedited by Carolyn Dinshaw of UC Berkeley. The Bay Area supports a thriving queer academic culture. Institutionally based queer scholars in the Bay Area include literary critic Terry Castle and historian Estelle Freedman at Stanford, art historian Jonathan Katz at CCSF, and French professor Leo Bersani at Berkeley. Community-based local scholars include Allan Bérubé, author of *Coming Out Under Fire,* a history of lesbians and gay men in World War II; Gayle Rubin, who has written trail-blazing essays on sexual politics and the anthropology of S/M since the 1970s; Will Roscoe, whose *Zuni Man-Woman* explores one particular Native American two-spirit tradition; Ellen Lewin, who wrote an influential study of lesbian mothers; and Eric Garber, author of numerous essays and anthologies on queer literary and historical topics. Other queer writers and activists support their work in the community as non-academic staff at Bay Area colleges. Chicana lesbian anthologist Carla Trujillo and GLAAD's Jessea Greenman both work at UC Berkeley, while Karl Knapper, president of the board of directors at Frameline, administers the Martin Luther King Papers Project at Stanford.

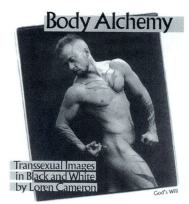

Body Alchemy

Transsexual Images in Black and White by Loren Cameron

God's Will

OPENING RECEPTION Monday May 1 • 7–10pm
Readings by James Green, David Harrison, Susan Stryker
at 7:30pm and 8:30pm
848 Community Art Space • For information: 415 / 765-7658
848 Divisadero (between Fulton & McAllister) in San Francisco
Opening Reception Admission: $5 (donation)
Gallery also OPEN: May 1–June 1, Sundays 1–5pm

Above: Photograph by Loren Cameron.

Judy Grahn shared keynote speaker honors with Allen Ginsberg at Out/Write 90: The First National Lesbian and Gay Writers Conference. *The successful conference, organized by Jeffrey Escoffier of* Out/Look *magazine, was held again in San Francisco the following year before relocating to Boston.*
Photograph by Rink Foto.

Out/Look *magazine, a national lesbian and gay quarterly published in San Francisco, made substantial contributions to queer intellectual, cultural, and political life during its all-too-brief existence from 1988 to 1992.*

Union. Although academics are sometimes thought to be disconnected from the "real world," queer scholarship has not simply reported on changing social conditions; it has actively participated in bringing about social change by transforming what we know of our own past as queer people and how we think about the role of sexuality in society. Establishing a queer presence on college campuses has been a form of grass-roots activism inside the ivory tower—a process through which queer faculty, students, staff, alumni, and interested members of the community have worked in an often antagonistic climate to open up academic opportunities for queer women and men, to offer more classes with relevant queer content, and to address the needs of queer employees who work in higher education. In the 1990s, San Francisco State, UC Berkeley, and New College in San Francisco have all established lesbian and gay studies programs. The Harvey Milk Institute, which opened its doors in 1995, is trying to be more successful at providing community-based continuing adult education for queers than the Lavender University, a similar institution that existed briefly in 1974.

Today's queer literary culture in the Bay Area is so rich that it defies any attempt to summarize it quickly. In recently published guides to contemporary lesbian and gay authors in the United States, nearly a quarter of the women and a fifth of the men had significant Bay Area connections. Simply listing names begins to sound like a Who's Who of contemporary American writing. In addition to people previously mentioned like Dorothy Allison, Gloria Anzaldua, Pat Califia, Armistead Maupin, Cherrie Moraga, and Pat Parker, other local figures include postmodern pastiche artists Steve Abbott and Kathy Acker; gay novelists Robert Glück, Bo Huston, Daniel Curzon, Paul Reed, Richard Hall, Fenton Johnson, and Kevin Killian; Native American storyteller Paula Gunn Allen; poets Adrienne Rich, Willyce Kim, Canyon Sam, Kitty Tsui, and Chrystos; bisexual feminist witch Starhawk; memoirist and vampire afficionada Jewelle Gomez; Filipina bad-girl novelist Chea Villanueva; *Another Mother Tongue* author Judy Grahn; lesbian mystery writers Katherine V. Forrest, Mabel Maney, and Mary Wings; as well as other talents like Susie Bright, Carol Queen, Terry Baum, Diane Bogus, Elana Dykewomon, Sally Gearhart, Susan Griffin, and Valerie Miner. Amy Scholder—an editor at City Lights since 1986—has been a powerful presence in the literary field with her High Risk imprint at Serpent's Tail Press in England. To help sustain and promote queer letters and publishing, the first Out/Write conferences were held in

San Francisco in 1990 and 1991. To continue meeting those needs locally after Out/Write relocated to Boston in 1992, Richard Labonté of A Different Light Bookstore sponsored the Readers and Writers conferences beginning in 1994.

A new generation of Bay Area writers is getting its start in the 'zines—small, irregularly distributed, cheaply produced underground periodical publications whose editors tend to think that occasionally turning a profit is only an added bonus to the thrill of disseminating their particular take on the world. The Bay Area has produced dozens of queer 'zines since the 1980s, when high-speed, high-quality photocopying and desktop publishing radically democratized print media. Lower costs enable people with highly specialized interests to target narrowly defined audiences—hence such publications as *Homoture, Black Sheets, Inciting Desire, Venus Castina, The Adventures of Baby Dyke, Outpunk, Whorezine, Slippery When Wet,* and other operations working on a minimal budget. A number of locally produced queer magazines with slightly more financial resources and higher production values have aimed for slightly wider audiences. *Frighten the Horses, Taste of Latex, Brat Attack,* and *Venus Infers* have all focused on radical sexuality; *Diseased Pariah News* caters to people with AIDS; *Girl Jock* and *Fat Girl* have self-explanatory names, while the more cryptically titled *Anything That Moves* addresses itself to bisexuals. At the top of the periodicals pyramid are local publications that have large national circulations like *Wilde,* the glossy men's magazine that debuted in 1995, *10 Percent,* the dyke-oriented *On Our Backs, Girlfriends,* and Franco Stephen's *Deneuve,* which claims a larger readership than any other lesbian publication in the world.

The twenty-fifth anniversary of the Stonewall Uprising was commemorated by exhibits throughout the Bay Area during the summer of 1994. The UC Berkeley Libraries sponsored O Pioneers! *to document a hundred years of homosexuality from 1894 to 1994. The San Francisco Public Library presented* Tales of the City, *a look at queer life in the Bay Area between 1969 and 1994. Two additional exhibits not shown here were* On the Edge of Revolt: Gays and Lesbians in San Francisco Before Stonewall, *curated at the Harvey Milk/Eureka Valley branch library by Ellen Meyers of the Gay and Lesbian Historical Society, and* From Passionate Friendship to Gay Liberation, *curated by Gerard Koskovich at Stanford University.* Graphic design by Mary Scott.

131

WHOREZINE

number
nineteen

movies 93
$3.00

The Magazine for Halloweeners and Inbetweeners

Dragazine

No. 0 $5.95

Gypsy
**The Lady
is a Camp!**

**Famed La Cage Emcee
Gets Aroused About**
Mel Brooks
Milton Berle
Joan Collins
Connie Francis
& How To Be (Or Not To Be)
A Well-Known Woman
Of Sorts, Sort of
Plus...
Enchanted by Philthee Ritz
Charmed by Dorian Corey
Swayed by Virginia Prince
Inspired by Wigstock '93
Stunned by Style Summit '93

*This Gown Ain't Big Enough
For The Both Of Us Issue*

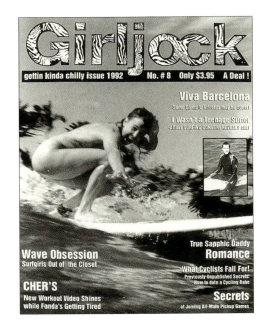

Girljock

gettin kinda chilly issue 1992   No. # 8   Only $3.95   A Deal !

Viva Barcelona
Some Olympic Athletes may be queer!

I Wasn't a Teenage Surfer
ADULT SURFING CONVERT REVEALS ALL!

Wave Obsession
Surfgirls Out of the Closet

CHER'S
New Workout Video Shines
while Fonda's Getting Tired

**True Sapphic Daddy
Romance**
What Cyclists Fall For!
Previously Unpublished Secrets:
How to date a Cycling Babe

Secrets
of Joining All-Male Pickup Games

BLACK SHEETS

a quarterly publication $5 US   Number

WARNING!
THIS ISSUE CONTAINS
SLEAZ
AND MAY OFFEND THOSE WHO
LACK A FIRM GRASP ON
REALITY!

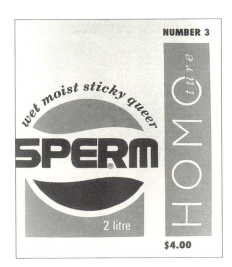

NUMBER 3

wet moist sticky queer

SPERM

HOMCuture

2 litre

$4.00

132

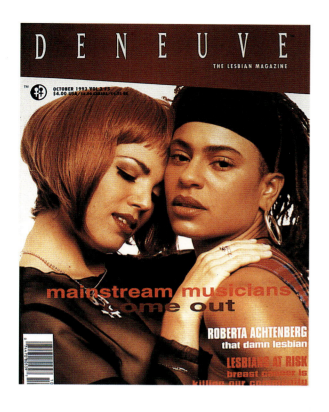

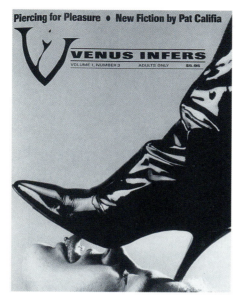

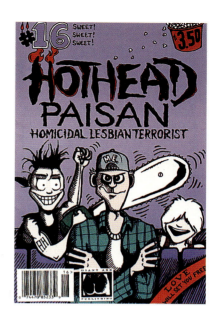

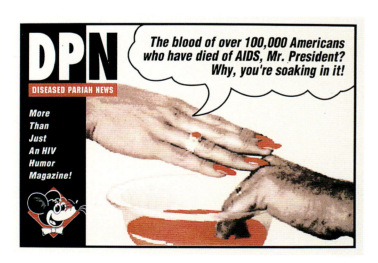

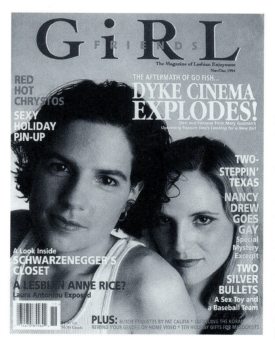

Bay Area Queer 'Zines and Periodicals.

Clockwise from left:
Whorezine
Dragazine
Deneuve
Venus Infers
Hothead Paisan
Girlfriends
DPN
Homoture
Black Sheets
Girljock

Photographs: Courtesy of GLHS.

Robert Mapplethorpe first visited San Francisco in 1968 "to find out if I'm gay once and for all." The trip represented a turning point; he returned to New York and immediately became involved with a young man. Mapplethorpe's 1978 photograph of S/M call boy "Elliot" was his first magazine cover and his only assignment for San Francisco-based Drummer, *edited by Jack Fritscher, who later chronicled Mapplethorpe's life in* Assault with a Deadly Camera. *Mapplethorpe's debut San Francisco exhibition in February 1979 at the Simon Lowinsky Gallery included flower studies, portraits, and a few relatively innocuous sex pictures. The next month* Censored, *featuring more explicit work that Mapplethorpe claimed was rejected for the previous show, opened at 80 Langton Street. A series of scatological images shot in a Sausalito boathouse were among those specifically targeted for censure during the 1989 1990 controversy over Mapplethorpe's NEA-funded retrospective.* Courtesy of GLHS.

Queer visual artists in the Bay Area are as prolific as their literary counterparts. Photographers like Freddy Niem, Greg Day, Mark Chester, Jill Posener, and Phyllis Christopher—as well as artists working in other media like Rodney Austin, David Dashiell, and Wayne Smith—have shown frequently in private spaces and such queer-friendly galleries as Southern Exposure, Morphos, Kiki, the LAB, and Eye Gallery. *In a Different Light,* Nayland Blake and Lawrence Rinder's engagingly idiosyncratic 1995 exhibit at Berkeley's University Art Museum, was the first major American museum retrospective to offer an in-depth assessment of how queers in the visual arts look at the world. It showcased the work of a number of artists with local ties—Rex Ray, J. John Priola, Catherine Opie, and Jerome Caja. The Bay Area has also sustained a tradition of queer film- and video-making since the days of the Queer Blue Light collective in the mid-1970s. Avant-garde filmmaker Barbara Hammer and *Sex Is...* director Marc Huestis have been working in the Bay Area for 20 years. Documentarian Debra Chasnoff earned an Oscar for her 1992 exposé of General Electric, *Deadly Deception,* and became the first queer person to explicitly acknowledge her lover at the Academy Awards ceremony. The controversy surrounding the late Marlon Riggs's video *Tongue's Untied,* an exploration of black gay identity, has overshadowed the UC Berkeley journalism professor's equally important works on race and AIDS, *Color Adjustment* and *Non Je Ne Regrette Rien.* Riggs's films continue to be distributed by Frameline, the organization that sponsors the annual San Francisco International Lesbian and Gay Film Festival. Under the artistic guidance of Mark Finch, Jenni Olson, Boone Nguyen, and Jennifer "Junkyard" Morris, the organization helped sustain a worldwide explosion of interest in the "New Queer Cinema" of the 1990s—a media trend analyzed by prominent local film critics Daniel Mangin and B. Ruby Rich.

Tony Kushner's award-winning two-part play *Angels in America,* which was commissioned by the Eureka Theatre of San Francisco in 1988, has been the most acclaimed work ever to emerge from the Bay Area's performing arts scene, but there have been many other fine pieces and performers. Pomo Afro Homos (Bernard Banner, Eric Gupton, and San Francisco Mime Troupe veteran Brian Freeman) broke new ground in the performing arts with their *Fierce Love* in 1991, which repeatedly played to rave reviews around the Bay Area before overcoming a homophobic reception in straight communities of color and reaching a wider audience. Pomo recent-addition Terrence Smith has become a regular feature at Josie's

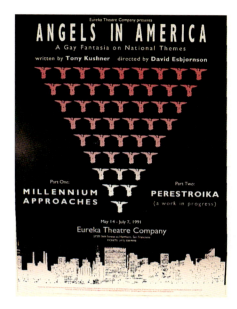

Far Left: *As the angel in Tony Kushner's Pulitzer Prize-winning play proclaims, "Heaven is a city much like San Francisco."* Millenium Approaches, *part one of the two-part "gay fantasia on national themes," and an early version of part two,* Perestroika, *premiered in May 1991 at San Francisco's Eureka Theatre.*

Left: *San Francisco filmmaker Debra Chasnoff acknowledged her lesbian relationship with life-partner Kim Klausner in front of millions of Academy Awards viewers when she won her best-documentary Oscar for* Deadly Deception *on March 30, 1992.* Courtesy of the Academy of Motion Picture Arts and Sciences.

Below: *Marlon Riggs and Essex Hemphill in* Tongues Untied (1989), *a searing exploration of black gay identity. When right-wing ideologues stole images from Riggs's video and recontextualized them in an anti-gay propaganda piece, Riggs sued and won.* Courtesy of Frameline.

Above: *Pat Bond, best known for her memorable appearance in Peter Adair's film* Word Is Out, *and for various one-woman shows, including* Conversations with Pat Bond *and* Gerty Gerty Stein is Back Back Back, *died of lung cancer in 1990 at age 65.* Courtesy of GLHS.

Right: *The gender-bending aesthetic of Los Angeles–based photographer Catherine Opie has deep roots in the Bay Area's leatherdyke community, as this portrait of Idexa demonstrates. Opie earned her BFA at the San Francisco Art Institute.* Photograph by Catherine Opie.

linda tillery
mary watkins
& bands

mills college
student union
friday, may 4
9pm – 1am
$4.⁰⁰

Linda Tillery Concert. Courtesy of GLHS.

Cabaret and Juice Joint with his "Late Night with Joan Jett Blakk," a live queer talk show hosted by the only out drag queen ever to run for president of the United States. Josie's has continued to be in the 1990s what the Valencia Rose was in the 1980s—a prestigious small club venue for local and national acts, like stand-up comics Suzy Berger and Mark Davis. Josie's increasingly has to vie with the multitude of small, queer-oriented performance galleries like Luna Sea and 848 Community Art Space that began to sprout up in the mid-1990s to showcase an abundance of fresh new local talent. One of the most innovative spaces has been Red Dora's Bearded Lady, a coffeehouse and cabaret that emerged from the same desire to create more women-oriented space that produced the Whiptail Lizard Lounge and its successor, Urban Womyn's Land. Bay Area queers have made equally diverse and vibrant contributions to contemporary musical performance. Respected classical composer Lou Harrison, San Francisco Symphony Orchestra conductor Michael Tilson Thomas, Kronos Quartet member Hank Dutt, drag diva Pussy Tourette, blues and folk singer Linda Tillery, hardcore pre-riot-grrrl rockers Tribe 8, and the dance club fags of Pansy Division all derive a measure of inspiration from the Bay Area's queer culture.

May 30, 1995.

Oakland native Glenn Burke, the only major league baseball player ever to reveal his homosexuality, died of AIDS in San Leandro just after his autobiography *Out at Home* went to press.

On April 21, 1994, demonstrators disrupted South of Market filming of Basic Instinct *in an attempt to pressure Hollywood for more accurate and balanced depictions of lesbians and gays.* Photograph by Rink Foto.

Queerness abounds in American culture in the 1990s to a degree unimaginable only a few years ago, and San Francisco Bay Area residents have helped shape the contours of often bitter conflicts over the relationship between sexual subcultures and national character and identity. Local dykes were quoted extensively in a June 23, 1993, *Newsweek* cover story on lesbianism, while the San Francisco chapter of the Gay and Lesbian Alliance Against Defamation (GLAAD) took the lead in protesting inaccurate depictions of homosexuality in mainstream films like *Basic Instinct*. Bill Clinton carried California in the 1992 presidential election due in part to fund-raising and campaigning on his behalf by many lesbians and gays who took heart in his anti-homophobic stance. One day after President-elect Clinton reaffirmed his pledge to lift the ban on homosexuals in the military, a federal court reinstated gay Air Force Petty Officer Keith Meinhold to his post at Moffet Field. When Congress balked at honoring Clinton's campaign promise and convened widely publicized hearings on gays in the military, works by Bay Area historian Allan Bérubé and journalist Randy Shilts informed those discussions. After retreating on the military issue and instituting the unsatisfactory "don't ask, don't tell" policy, Clinton tried to appease his gay Bay Area constituency with the appointment of San Francisco City Supervisor Roberta Achtenberg to the position of Assistant Secretary for Fair Housing and

Cast members of MTV's Real World, *a popular show in which a group of strangers agree to live together for several months and to allow their interactions to be filmed. Sean Sasser (second from right) and Pedro Zamora (far right) were lovers before Pedro died of AIDS.* Photograph by Rick Gerharter/Impact Visuals.

June 3, 1993.

Former San Francisco Supervisor Roberta Achtenberg sworn in as Assistant Secretary for Fair Housing and Equal Opportunity, becoming the highest-ranking open lesbian to serve in the federal government. Photograph by Rick Gerharter/Impact Visuals.

Clubs come and go in San Francisco, but DJs like Page Hodel have real staying power. Pictured are Lewis Walden and Michael Blue of Chaos and Club Uranus, two of the more popular nightspots in the 1990s, which also include the Box, Pleasuredome, Muff Dive, Junk, Klubstitute, and G-Spot.
Photograph by Daniel Nicoletta.

Equal Opportunity—making her the highest-ranking open lesbian ever to serve in the federal government. Clinton subsequently distanced himself from queer issues, failing to support the nomination of gay San Francisco philanthropist James C. Hormel for a diplomatic post.

For all the many achievements in which the queer community of the San Francisco Bay Area can justly take pride, our future is by no means secure. Californians thus far have been spared the likes of anti-queer Proposition 9 in Oregon or Amendment 2 in Colorado, but we still face active discrimination. Foreshadowing his later opposition to affirmative action, on September 29, 1991, Governor Pete Wilson vetoed Assembly Bill 101, a law banning employment discrimination on the basis of sexual orientation. Police violence continues to be a

140

Left: *The Cafe Flore, San Francisco's quintessential queer cafe on Market near Castro, is the preferred place to just hang out when not trying to change the world. Pictured are John Major, left, and Bob Smith.* Photograph by Daniel Nicoletta.

Below: *Gay Asian-Pacific Alliance (GAPA) and Asian-Pacific Sisters (APS) participated in the San Francisco Chinese New Year parade on February 26, 1994, the first time Asian gay and lesbian groups marched openly in a Chinese New Year parade. On April 24, 1994, the two groups, joined by Older Asian Sisters in Solidarity (OASIS) and the GAPA Community HIV Project (GCHP), wore lavender headbands and hapi coats as they became the first overtly queer Asian contingent to march in the Japanese community's annual Cherry Blossom Parade.* Photograph by Rick Gerharter/Impact Visuals.

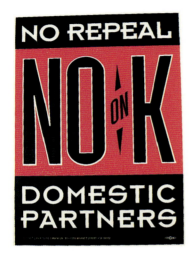

Roberto Esteves and Uwe Damerow were among the first of over 275 lesbian and gay couples to register at City Hall on Valentine's Day in 1991 after San Francisco's domestic partnership referendum went into effect. Measure K was an unsuccessful attempt later that year to overturn the referendum.

Photograph by Rink Foto.

serious problem, as the January 1, 1995, raid on a Visual AID benefit party made clear. Without a search warrant, more than 40 SFPD officers entered the private residence where the event was being held, beat guests, and confiscated property. The charges against party organizers were later dropped, and the raid became the subject of a class-action lawsuit. Besides contending with willful acts of other human beings, we are also faced with an array of problems larger than any one group of people can cause or cure—AIDS and breast cancer epidemics, anti-abortion fanaticism, homelessness, and immigration hysteria. New issues will undoubtedly continue to appear. But not all of the problems within the community can be attributed to hostile outsiders or forces beyond our control. We remain a profoundly divided community caught up in a wildly contradictory present, separated from each other by race, class, gender, and political persuasion. We seem poised between utopian fantasies of a bloodless lavender revolution and scary images of Berlin after Hitler's rise to power, with no consensus likely to emerge about the best course to chart into an uncertain future.

The present moment is the inescapable standpoint from which we envision our pasts and whatever future we strive to build. A sober optimism seems to characterize our queer here and now. In spite of mounting premillennial anxieties and the often harsh realities of day-to-day life in this beautiful city and its environs,

Governor Pete Wilson's veto on September 29, 1991, of State Assembly Bill 101,
a law banning employment discrimination on the basis of sexual orientation,
sparked demonstrations in San Francisco. Photograph by Rink Foto.

Breast cancer has reached epidemic proportions in the 1990s, as the baby-boom generation settles into middle age. The National Women's Cancer Resource Center in Berkeley provides information and assistance to lesbians and other women. Photograph © by Cathy Cade.

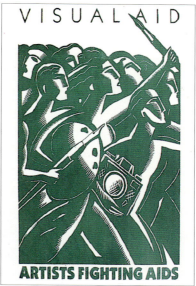

Above: *A benefit party for Visual AID, an organization devoted to assisting PWAs with their visual arts projects, was raided by SFPD officers on January 1, 1995, provoking outcries of police brutality and resulting in a class-action lawsuit filed on behalf of the attendees.*

Left: *Jessea Greenman of the Gay and Lesbian Alliance Against Defamation (GLAAD) confronts opponents of Project 10, a state-funded program for addressing queer issues in California high schools. GLAAD's San Francisco office benefited from the leadership of dynamic executive director Tom Di Maria between 1993 and 1995.* Photograph by Rick Gerharter/Impact Visuals.

October 6, 1992.

The City Library Commission voted 5-1 to continue flying the rainbow flag over the Eureka Valley-Harvey Milk Memorial Branch Library after the flag (donated in 1989 by the gay Alexander Hamilton Post of the American Legion) became the focus of a homophobic attack by the Christian Coalition.

Queer activism in the 1990s means paying attention to the ways various social issues like homelessness, substance use, immigration, and abortion intersect. Rebecca Hensler (left) and Ingrid Nelson (holding microphone) speaking at the Women's Demonstration outside the 6th International Conference on AIDS. Photograph by Daniel Nicoletta.

one sees hopeful signs of a commitment to better times ahead. The concerns of queer and questioning youth—our community of tomorrow—are receiving more attention than they ever have, and we are in the midst of a veritable baby boom, as record numbers of lesbians and gay men choose to parent. This impulse to actively build a future for ourselves and our loved ones seems directly related to the current heightened level of concern for our collective past. As it has in so many other areas of endeavor, San Francisco has taken an important first step in preserving and investigating queer history. Supported by bonds approved by San Francisco voters in 1988 and formally announced by Mayor Art Agnos on October 10, 1991, the Gay and Lesbian Center of the new main library will be the world's first permanent research center in a public institution specifically devoted to the documentation of queer history and culture.

We all live in spaces secured for us by those who came before, and will leave the world for those who follow. This book is dedicated to all the queer people of the San Francisco Bay Area—past, present, and future—whose lives constitute a story worth telling and preserving.

The Deaf Gay & Lesbian Center (DGLC), founded in March 1992, was the first social service program in the country to focus exclusively on the unique needs of deaf queers. Its logo is the American Sign Language sign for "support." Dragonsani "Drago" Renteria, who became DGLC Director shortly after its founding, also publishes the national CTN Magazine for deaf queers and in June 1995 became the first deaf person ever to be Grand Marshal of a major pride parade. Courtesy of Drago Renteria.

The National Center for Lesbian Rights, located in San Francisco, has been a strong advocate for the rights of lesbians to conceive or adopt children. The Lyon-Martin Women's Health Clinic offers innovative parenting education classes for lesbian and bisexual women. Photograph © by Cathy Cade.

"You are not alone as PUNKS, QUEERS, and more importantly as YOUTH OF THIS COUNTRY. They keep throwing on our faces that we are the future and we need to prepare for it. This coming from people who will tell us how to screw to get some one pregnant but won't tell us to use a condom . . . Frankly that's bullshit and all of us know it. We are not getting anything from the school system because they fail to recognize the FACT that we exist . . . Let's do something about this. Like, oh, I don't know, maybe a walkout of the bay area schools on let's say, ohhhh, October 11, 1991, maybe. Sound like a plan? . . . So until the uprising, remember when your family, friends, any one, gives you shit about who and what you are just tell them or just tell yourself that 'WE ARE YOUR SONS AND DAUGHTERS AND WE ARE NOT ALONE!!!!!'" (signed) QUEER YOUTH PUNK TYPE PERSON

—anonymous photocopied flyer
distributed in the Bay Area, 1991.

Photograph by Rick Gerharter/Impact Visuals.

1-800-246-PRIDE
outside the 415 area
code

TDD#: 415/431-8812

The LYRIC Youth
Talkline is a peer
support and
information line for
gay, lesbian,
bisexual transgender
and questioning
youth under 24.

415/863-3636

I JUST KISSED ANOTHER WOMAN!

I THINK I AM A WOMAN...

©TSAPP93

Opposite page: *The Red Balloon squat on Polk Street during the summer of 1993 received national news coverage and called attention to the plight of queer street youth in San Francisco.* Photograph by Jason Albertson.

Top Left: *In 1993, the San Francisco chapter of the Lesbian Avengers sponsored the first annual Dyke March, whose slogan, "We're not waiting for the Rapture, We are the Apocalypse," sums up the mood of many queer people at the close of the 20th century.* Lesbian Avengers logo courtesy of GLHS.

Top Right: *LYRIC (Lavendar Youth Recreation Information Center) advertisement, 1995.* Courtesy of Terry Sapp.

1993.

Tom Rielly and Karen Wickre of Digital Queers helped get the National Gay and Lesbian Task Force online, and have worked diligently to help many local San Francisco queer groups communicate on the Internet.

Left: *A new generation of queers have their own self-conscious uses and abuses for history.* Photograph by Daniel Nicoletta.

151

Members of the Women's Motorcycle Contingent better known as Dykes on Bikes roar into the future as they pass by the construction site of the Gay and Lesbian Center in the new main San Francisco Public Library, 1994. Photograph by Rick Gerharter/Impact Visuals.

Bibliography

$\mathcal{A}$ work like *Gay by the Bay* requires the use of many different kinds of source material, both primary (directly produced by the events being discussed) and secondary (produced later by scholars and other writers). Rather than list all the various sources consulted, we have chosen to direct readers interested in exploring the Bay Area's queer history in greater depth to the places where research materials can be found, and to mention only a few of the more useful secondary works.

The archival holdings of the Gay and Lesbian Historical Society (GLHS) of Northern California are the richest and most accessible source for queer history in the Bay Area. In addition to hundreds of periodicals published locally since the 1950s, the GLHS has queer newspapers and magazines from all over the country. It holds scores of manuscript collections, both from individuals and organizations, and it has literally thousands of photographs, videotapes, posters, flyers, matchbook covers, lapel pins, and other sorts of ephemera. Those collections most useful for this book were the Periodicals Collection, the Guy Strait Newspaper Collection, the Ephemera Collection, the Photographic Collections, and the papers of Elsa Gidlow, Lou Sullivan, Ralph Greene, Phyllis Lyon and Del Martin, the Council on Religion and the Homosexual, the Tavern Guild, Henry Dieckoff, Pat Bond, Crawford Barton, Valencia Rose, ACT-UP, Robert Chesley, Akimbo, and Queer Nation. *Our Stories: The Newsletter of the Gay and Lesbian Historical Society of Northern California,* published irregularly two to four times a year since 1985, contains many reprints of important historical documents and oral histories in the GLHS collections.

The San Francisco History Room Photographic Archives in the San Francisco Main Library were an especially useful resource. We also made limited use of what promises to be another truly important body of material that was not yet fully accessible at the time we were working on this book—the collections of the library's Gay and Lesbian Center. Those collections we were able to access were the Barbara Grier and Donna McBride Collection, the Randy Shilts Collection, the Peter Adair/*Word Is Out* Collection and the ephemera vertical files.

The Bancroft Library at the University of California at Berkeley has one of the best collections of Western Americana in the world, including primary source material on the San Francisco Bay Area. There are no collections on the history of sexuality per se, but there is a great deal of relevant material dispersed throughout their holdings—for example, papers of queer UC student groups, or the papers of literary figures like Gertrude Stein and Robert Duncan. Stanford's Greene Library houses a growing collection of queer material, including the papers of Allen Ginsberg. Other important sources can be found in the holdings of the California Historical Society in San Francisco. The June Mazer Collection at the University of Southern California, which incorporated the defunct Women's History Archive in Berkeley in the early 1980s, has a great deal of material on Bay Area lesbian history.

In contrast to the rich variety of primary source material, there is a startling paucity of published writing on local queer history—only a handful of short works and as yet no book-length study other than this one. Listed below are the works we found useful, as well as a few titles of related interest that help provide a broader context for understanding North American queer history in the 19th and 20th centuries. Those items from which we drew specific quotes are referenced in the body of the text.

BÉRUBÉ, ALLAN. *Coming Out Under Fire: The History of Gay Men and Women in World War II.* New York: Macmillan, 1990.

————. "The History of the Gay Bathhouse." *Coming Up!,* vol. 6, no. 3 (1984): 15–19.

BOYD, NAN ALAMILLA. "San Francisco Was a Wide Open Town." Ph.D. diss., Brown University, 1995 (forthcoming from University of California Press).

CHAUNCEY, GEORGE. *Gay New York: Gender, Urban Culture, and the Making of the Gay Male World, 1890–1940.* New York: Basic Books, 1994.

D'EMILIO, JOHN. *Making Trouble: Essays on Gay History, Politics, and the University.* New York: Routledge, 1992.

————. *Sexual Politics, Sexual Communities: The Making of a Homosexual Minority in the United States, 1940–1970.* Chicago and London: University of Chicago Press, 1983.

————. "Gay Politics, Gay Community: San Francisco's Experience." *Socialist Review,* no. 55 (1981).

D'EMILIO, JOHN, and ESTELLE FREEDMAN. *Intimate Matters: A History of Sexuality in America.* New York: Harper & Row, 1988.

DUBERMAN, MARTIN BAUML, MARTHA VICINUS, and GEORGE CHAUNCEY, EDS. *Hidden from History: Reclaiming the Gay and Lesbian Past.* New York: New American Library, 1989.

GIDLOW, ELSA. *Elsa: I Come with My Songs: The Autobiography of Elsa Gidlow.* San Francisco: Booklegger Press & Druid Heights Books, 1986.

HALE, EDWARD EVERETT. *The Queen of California.* San Francisco: Colt Press, 1945.

KATZ, JONATHAN NED. *Gay/Lesbian Almanac: A New Documentary.* New York: Carroll & Graf, 1994.

LEGRAND, TOTO [LOU RAND HOGAN]. "The Golden Age of the Queens." *Bay Area Reporter,* a six-part series beginning September 1974.

Lyon, Phyllis, and Del Martin. *Lesbian/Woman.* New York: Bantam, 1972.

Morrisroe, Patricia. *Mapplethorpe: A Biography.* New York: Random House, 1995.

Samois. *Coming to Power: Writings and Graphics on Lesbian S/M.* Palo Alto: UpPress, 1981.

Shilts, Randy. *And the Band Played On: Politics, People and the AIDS Epidemic.* New York: St. Martin's Press, 1987.

————. *Mayor of Castro Street: The Life and Times of Harvey Milk.* New York: St. Martin's Press, 1982.

Smith-Rosenberg, Carol. "The Female World of Love and Ritual." In *Disorderly Conduct: Visions of Gender in Victorian America.* New York: A. A. Knopf, 1985.

Solnit, Rebecca. *Secret Exhibition: Six California Artists of the Cold War Era.* San Francisco: City Lights Books, 1990.

Sullivan, Louis G. *From Female to Male: The Life of Jack B. Garland.* Boston: Alyson, 1990.

Index